AWAKENING TO AUTHENTICITY COLLECTION

GROWING INTO YOU & GROWING STRONGER: FIND PURPOSE, CULTIVATE INNER PEACE AND STAND OUT BY BECOMING THE BEST VERSION OF YOURSELF

Y.D. GARDENS

THE EMERALD SOCIETY

Editor's note:

This publication is not intended as a substitute for the advice of health care professionals.

JUST FOR YOU

Follow the link below to download your FREE copy:
www.emeraldsocpublishing.com

Awakening
TO
AUTHENTICITY COLLECTION
GROWING INTO YOU & GROWING STRONGER:
FIND PURPOSE, CULTIVATE INNER PEACE AND STAND OUT
Growing
STRONGER
Y. D. GARDENS
Growing
INTO YOU
Y.D.GARDENS
Y.D. GARDENS

PART I

GROWING INTO YOU

DEDICATION

To Matt: Your authenticity has always amazed and inspired me. Thank you for showing me that the road less travelled is also beautiful.

FOREWORD

As far as I can remember, I have always been curious about the wonders of the world. During my early adulthood, I became an avid traveler, backpacking through foreign countries, exploring the vast mystery beyond borders. I can recall a particular day in 2014 when I journeyed across several Central American countries. I had just stepped back into Mexico following an adventurous few days, crossing dodgy borders without much more than my Canadian passport and a backpack filled with my most essential belongings.

I stayed with a *couchsurfer* friend who was hosting my travel mates and myself for a few nights. As we unpacked some of our belongings and settled in for some much-needed rest, I noticed that the bedroom walls were bare, except for this one wall hanging. It was a framed, thin strip of cardboard on which one could read:

"*What would you attempt if you knew you could not fail?*"

This provoking statement has stuck with me to this day. I believe there comes a time in life when we must question if we are living up to our full potential. What could we change to create our best, most fulfilling life? I wondered about the extent of that statement. How often do we make ourselves the only obstacle standing in our way to happiness? How often do our thought patterns prevent us from achieving our goals? How do limiting beliefs influence our life path, how we perceive our world, and how we view ourselves?

I began to question, research, and observe others – most of all, I took a deep dive into myself. Introspection can go a long way, revealing the good, the bad, and much ugliness. As I began working on this manuscript, I realized that I was always offering to others all of which I was withholding from myself: credibility, kindness, compassion, love, and respect. I was unintentionally depriving myself of the most valuable tools to achieve a well-rounded, fulfilling life.

From the moment I fully came to this realization, I started to observe my reactions towards my environment mindfully. I was shocked at how destructive and self-deprecating my ingrained thought patterns truly were. How had I become like this? And more importantly, how was I meant to break through and move past these hindering thoughts and behaviors?

Weeks went by as I wrote and dove into research. I eventually came to realize that I was growing simultaneously with the advancement of this book. Chapter by chapter, I was rethinking what I thought I knew and applying the strategies more consciously than ever before. Writing *Growing Into You* has been a blessing in disguise. I have come to a new understanding of how crucial it is to stand proudly within yourself and expose your truth. I genuinely hope that as you flip through these pages you will feel, as I did, increasingly empowered to move towards your goals, stand your ground, and be authentic.

Although no large amounts of blood or sweat were shed in this book's writing, I can assure you that it has brought its lot of emotional triggers and reflections. The ups and downs of creating such a self-challenging piece of work have provided much insight into my own life. I have kept myself from writing for many years, mostly from fear of revealing myself entirely. As you may know, expression through art exposes us to great vulnerability. Ironically, while creating every chapter of this book, I've had to fight my instinctive urge to avoid exposing my truth. I persisted, fighting my conditioned inner resistance. I did end up finding enough strength to power through; I fought my battle up to the very last page.

Every story is worth sharing, and we are connected in more ways than we can perceive.

Finally, I created this first book as food for thought. It is a first step and the foundational work towards understanding how to grow into ourselves and stand strong while embracing all that we are. From psychology to spirituality, there is an abundance of aspects that influence who we are as a whole and who we choose to become. I wrote *Growing Into You* to tackle the most influential factors and provide some insight into embarking upon the next steps of your journey. *The Well-Being Handbook,* as well as the sequel *Growing Stronger,* offers more in-depth advice and tools as you progress on your path. Each of these is a valuable asset in exploring various topics as you grow and gain more understanding of the fundamental concepts related to self.

Beyond all, I wish for these words to bring you comfort

in knowing that you are acknowledged and supported throughout your journey. I hope you realize that you are not alone; authenticity is a life-long voyage, and we are all in this together.

Let's stand tall. Let's stand proud. Let's stand just as we are.

PREFACE

The Calling

Long ago, when my spirit was untainted,
I danced to my own rhythm and ran at my own pace
Blindly awaiting a verdict
As to how to follow the stream,
One that would soon lead me astray from my dream.

They claimed running was not for me,
My body too weak to take me where I should go.
I followed blindly, but little did I know
That my mind would soon forget how to flow.

Every step was weighed, success charted in grades;
I ran for him and for her,
I was running to my grave.

I ran to comply, I ran to achieve,

A race that was never mine;
Undeceiving, I ran as others pleased
Every single time.

Then, one day, the entire world paused,
Humanity kept to themselves for a cause,
And as patterns and long ingrained thoughts receded
I attempted to run without feeling defeated.

This time I could stop and knew I could rest;
I no longer felt being judged by a test.
Step by step, ahead and forward I went;
Unburdened, I took off without any intent.

I soared through the air, the wind in my hair.
This day was mine to seize, and old boundaries to tear.
As the rays heated my skin and warmed my soul,
I sped forward for freedom; not for a goal.

I had not stepped out in years,
How could I have been stronger?
Yet through the free flow of tears
I moved faster, and ran further.

As goose bumps rose and prickled my arms,
I knew at once they had lied;
I refused to surrender to success or charm,
This race had never been governed by pride.
It had never been about distance or pace;
The rhythm of my heart was the ultimate chase.

If I'd ignored the voices, perhaps I'd have learnt sooner
That following the crowd

Would never make me a winner.
For the battle is inside
And is our own to fight;
At our pace, it is our race -
And only we know what's right.

INTRODUCTION

Through the ages, we have grown as a people because of our ability to learn from others. We are well versed at reading op-ed pieces from industry giants, reading memoirs from great leaders, and soaking up as much as we can from the opinions of intellectual titans.

As human beings, we have created complex and intricate economic and governmental systems because of our ability to study our environment, learn from it, and use this knowledge to better our lives. We have put so much into learning, knowing, and improving the world, mainly from what we learn from observing our surroundings, that it is surprising that we have not extended that same courtesy back to ourselves. Many of us have failed to learn to know ourselves. We have been unable to respect our veritable nature and to grow into it fully and authentically. How did this result come about?

Human beings run from pain for most of their lives, whether consciously or instinctively; it is in our nature to avoid suffering. We may have witnessed others make the mistake of running away from what could have been their source of liberation simply because they chose comfort and security over authenticity. They have become comfortable with a friendly version of themselves that they know, instead of facing the challenges of unearthing the version of themselves that is more fulfilled than their current state.

You see, it is normal to want to avoid pain. However, pain is vital to growth. It is merely a signal that something, somewhere, isn't right. If you experience much pain in your life on various levels, it is most likely an indicator that the life path you are following is not your main road to fulfillment. You may have been and are possibly still avoiding something. It is a signal that something has to be altered or fixed in your life before change and progress can begin to take place. Our learning and evolution can only happen when we make an effort to explore and reflect on it.

Avoiding something that is a crucial and vital aspect of your inner composition – the essence of your reason for being – may lead to many consequences. Repressing your innermost wants and needs by refusing to acknowledge them can affect you emotionally, psychologically, and physically. The whole of your being is interconnected; negligence of one aspect ultimately affects your entire entity. The beauty, however, lies in the fact that the choice to change is always yours. You can decide to keep avoiding whatever you refuse to face and continue to take the ever-increasing pain that comes as a result. However, suppose you can find the courage to change your relationship with pain and seek further, to look into the underlying issues causing this suffering and work out how you can stop it. In that case, the life-changing benefits will be immense.

Unfortunately, most of us must hit the final hurdle before

summoning the strength to face the discomfort. Avoiding suffering is such a powerful and innate component of our being. Often, it is only when we have nothing else to lose that we can face the depth of our emotional turmoil. The moment we decide that enough is enough and that we cannot take it anymore, the doorway to our salvation bursts open.

Many of us fail to realize that avoiding pain is not the same as dealing with it. This concept may seem simple enough; however, most of these mechanisms, operated by our subconscious mind, act in ways to protect us. As we instinctively use continual avoidance, our true nature becomes buried under layers of unsubstantial and superficial societal adaptive means. That little voice in our heads, our mind's narrator, seemingly becomes part of who we think we are. Ultimately, this can only lead to a situation where the pain will accumulate to a level where it becomes impossible to avoid or escape.

As many of us live under the illusion and fantasy that by running away from pain, it will magically go away, it can often come as a surprise to discover the extent of the damage we have done to ourselves. As such a low point occurs, one must realize that only one solution remains: face the music and leap headfirst into a journey of recovery. This is not an easy path, as it requires much personal investment, determination, resilience, patience, and vulnerability. It implies discovering how much harm our own ego can inflict upon our authentic nature, and how this impacts our wellbeing. However, through detachment and observation, we can take on this challenge. By doing the work and confronting ourselves, we can unravel our essence and reconnect with our innermost self.

You can have a million and one experiences, but at the end of it all, it always comes back to yourself. There is no escaping it; that dormant entity that fills and consumes your being behind all the misconceptions, traumas, failures, and losses you have faced is always within. The you that is lying motionless behind all the closed doors is waiting for salvation. You are behind the loss of your peace, meaning, and natural-born state, all of which you have forgotten. You are the only one accountable for yourself.

There is no escape outside of embracing self, and anyone who tells you otherwise is not only lying to you but also themselves. Again, avoidance cannot lead to healing. No matter how happy you think you are, you can never be truly complete until you face your truth.

The problem isn't the methods to use or the means to employ or the book to study to gain the necessary knowledge; the problem lies in whether we choose to accept the pain. The moment you consciously decide to face the hard facts and commence the journey to find yourself, you have already taken a step forward in opening yourself up to discomfort, which leads to revelations. You have now manifested that you are ready to make an effort to know who you are, even though unpleasant revelations might cover the truth. Being prepared to delve into introspection can be very painful. It may imply unleashing certain prevalent self-deceptions, such as having to own up to your life choices and accept that you are the only one responsible for your life and perceptions. It is about taking responsibility for your actions and working through the struggle of assuming the role we play in how our life unfolds.

You are always free to choose your thoughts. You can easily opt for lying to yourself about weaknesses and decide that the problem isn't with you but the world, that you're right and the others are wrong, or even that you don't need to change to achieve your goals but that the whole world needs to do better.

If you decide you are ready for change, you must be prepared to accept the pain instead of running from it, as you've done for so long. It is impossible to change something we cannot see. By exploring this discomfort, you can begin to heal and better yourself. It is only by being open about who you are, where you are, and where you want to be that you can improve.

The easy way out is choosing to remain the same person that you were yesterday. It is to convince yourself that there is no point in opting for the painful path of discovering your true self; instead, you might decide to settle for where you are right now. What is difficult and painful is to embrace the pain that comes from being vulnerable, to accept the possibility of being wrong, and to face the reality of how things are instead of living a fantasy.

The world's history is filled with stories of successful people who chose to work through psychological discomfort to better themselves and achieve their goals. They overcame obstacles and enjoyed their life with graceful ease, leaving their mark on the world because they embraced the painful unknown rather than the sweet familiar.

Why exactly do we need to know ourselves? Without knowing oneself, it is impossible to lead a complete, balanced, and fulfilling existence. The quest of a lifetime is the search for one's true self. As you simultaneously connect back to your essence and the winds of life bring about change, your feet will remain steadily grounded. Environmental and social factors will no longer shake you. You will know where you stand, firmly and proudly, confidently laying down the boundaries to your well-rounded existence. Self-awareness allows us to connect to the knowledge of specific life-enhancing attributes and capabilities. Leaving your true self buried may make you prone to incidences of mistaken ambitions, low self-esteem, poor quality of life through making choices that do not align with your innermost desires, and misplacement of priorities.

You are about to embark upon a unique journey into yourself. The time has come to turn inwards, and, if you choose to do so, to work through the hurdles. Turn inwards, deep into the essence of your being. What is so special about knowing ourselves? Are there any dangers in lacking self-knowledge? How important is it that we learn to understand who we are at the very source? What are the different avenues through which we can begin to unfold our truth and grow into ourselves? Many questions will arise on your path to self-discovery as you wonder about how to lead your journey to authentic living and towards becoming YOU. You are your solution; all answers lie within your true self.

1

GROWING INTO YOUR SELF

> "One of the greatest tragedies in life is to lose your own sense of self and accept the version of you that is expected by everyone else."
>
> — K.L. Toth

Socrates, great philosopher of ancient Greece, once made the famous declaration: "man know thyself." This Athenian philosopher gained much wisdom and knowledge through exploring the depths of this statement. Having a sense of self is as essential today as it was in his time, if not more. It plays a crucial role in our lives. Living without a holistically connected sense of self is not living, but merely existing.

The consequences of neglecting one's intrinsically profound identity are vast. A 2017 report published by the

United States National Institute of Mental Health showed that an estimated 46.6 million (an equivalence of 18.9%) American adults battle mental illness. Even more alarming is the fact that less than half of these cases received professional help. This implies that almost 20 million residents of the United States were unable or failed to seek help to get a better grip on their life and sense of self. Anxiety disorders, impulse control disorders, mood disorders, and substance use disorders are only a few of the increasingly frequent ailments plaguing our modern society and hindering our development and wellbeing.

Psychologists have stated that a lack of sense of self is responsible for many addictive and compulsive behaviors. They posit that the early patterns of suppressing and ignoring our feelings instead of expressing, communicating, and accepting them are predominant factors and sources of compulsion and dependency.

Let's understand that these mental conditions vary in severity, and so not all of them are about significant mental issues such as depression, schizophrenia, and OCD (obsessive-compulsive disorder). However, that still does not remove from the equation that we must seek to gain a sense of self, a strong one at that, or risk falling into modern social norms, thus becoming another addition to the mental disorder statistics. It is in our power to develop a strong and infallible self-identity. Living beneath your actual value and not rising to your full potential is a tragic disservice to yourself. You do not have to live a life that is not fully and truly yours. The power to generate change is in your hands.

Sense of Self

First and foremost, let's attempt to define sense of self. What is self or sense of self, and how can you build a healthy self-image? In simple terms, your sense of self is your identity: a fusion between who you think you are and what you convey to the outside world. It is your perception of yourself that leads you to make decisions and guide your life path. How you feel about yourself, your thought patterns, your level of self-esteem, and your confidence or lack thereof directly correlate to your sense of self.

Challenges are an inevitable part of life. Our sense of self or self-image plays a predominant role in establishing our response to adversity. When our sense of self is weak, and these unfavorable circumstances come knocking, we may quickly become overwhelmed by them, no matter how big or small the challenge appears. Let's look at it this way: picture a nice boat floating effortlessly at sea. The weather is beautiful, the breeze gentle, and the warm sun gently caresses your skin. Then suddenly, you notice the scenery shift: the wind becomes increasingly tortuous, the water wildly turbulent, and now the boat is being tossed about, leaving you to fend for yourself. However, you find you can breathe calmly, and you feel safe in knowing that the previously reinforced mainsail will stir you in the right direction and that the sturdy structure of your boat will keep you afloat, no matter the power of the storm.

As you've probably guessed, this boat represents our sense of self, just as the choppy waters and unpredictable winds mirror the struggles of life. Challenges are inevitable and, therefore, will always present themselves to you. However, a healthy self-image and sense of identity will provide a solid foundation for creating a life that reflects your genuine thoughts, opinions, wants, and needs. The reason you will come out unscathed and even stronger than before whenever you face challenges is that you have armed yourself with a strong sense of self. Some obstacles may leave you soaked with water or flunked around by stormy winds, but knowing the strength of your sails, you will have confidence in the depth of your power. You will have set clear boundaries and hold a firm grasp on what you are willing to let into your life. People will know who you are and where you stand.

We are nothing without identity. It is a crucial aspect of our human composition because it is what defines who we are. It outlines our life path, acknowledging where we are and dictating where we are headed. Sense of self is so wide-reaching that it will influence every area of your life. The way you perceive who you are will affect the things you believe about yourself (because yes, everything is a mere perception), the world around you, and your place in it. In simple terms, changing your mindset can alter your sense of self and essentially change your entire life.

This is why living with an underdeveloped sense of self can be very damaging. Chronic stress, anxiety, and depression are a few indicators that your self-image may need some dusting off or even a complete makeover. Signs of a low or underdeveloped sense of self may manifest through agreeing to do things you don't want to do. You might find yourself missing out on significant opportunities because of an inability to be decisive, have a constant feeling of inadequacy, engage in negative self-talk, and continually try to please everyone - to your detriment. These are all choices that sacrifice your wellbeing and ultimately lead to forging a life that is not authentically yours.

Depending on the strength of your sense of self and your perception of who you are, answers to the questions "Who are you?" or "What defines who you are?" will vary. Some might talk about their roles as mothers; others might answer by stating their area of work or professional expertise; some others might talk about their relationships and the roles they play in them, such as being a supportive friend, a present mother, or a caring daughter. Some choose to define themselves by their personality traits, such as easy-going, fun, hard-working, or intelligent. The answers we give are not entirely factual but rather a representation of who we think we are. Understand that this sense of self is something we developed very early in life. It has been tainted by experiences and trauma and, for most, solidified in emotional scar tissue as we advanced through life. Consequently, as we age and go through life-transforming incidents, they must also evolve and adjust to fit our self-concept.

Why develop a strong sense of self?

All aspects of your life - the holistic threadwork of your existence - are laid upon the foundation of your sense of self. A strong sense of self brings about confidence and ambition and helps to distinguish you from others. As humans, we are physiologically, biologically, spiritually, mentally, and emotionally wired to strive and flourish under certain circumstances. The substructure consists of an accurately defined and well-balanced self-image and identity.

Firstly, there is a distinction between having a weak sense of self and having no sense of self at all. One is based on a faulty perception of self-worth, while the latter is often triggered by trauma occurring over periods of childhood and adolescence, resulting in a lack of or inexistence of self-identity. In either case, the impact may be a substantial lack of understanding of yourself as an individual. You may feel out of place or lost in society, perhaps empty and purposeless, weak, dependent, and lose faith in your ability to grow into a well-rounded version of yourself. In this case, it is not uncommon to continually seek outside approval and self-worth from others. The brain-fog can be so weighty and impairing that you may have no idea where your potential lies, let alone what you are capable of accomplishing.

If you do not know who you are or perhaps have an altered perception of yourself, you will struggle with managing your priorities, setting goals for your life, and being able to separate what you want from what you don't. Why? Because you have no idea who you truly are, and so cannot decide what your life should resemble. This can easily lead to a stream of misdirected life choices, which can only amount to a dissatisfying life situation. How can one possibly expect to achieve their goals and fulfill their ambitions if they don't know what they truly want?

Perhaps a need to pause, reflect, and face the hard truths of your journey this far will be beneficial. When you don't know where you are or where you came from, it is almost impossible to pinpoint where you are going.

As such, your sense of self should be continually assessed and maintained, just as you would your car, your job, your body, and your relationships. After all, it is the foundation of all aspects governing your life choices. You can do this by tuning in and listening to your thought patterns, observing your habits and behaviors, and contemplating how you respond to your environment. As you read on, you will see yourself offered more food for thought, as well as several tools to help you embark upon this process.

It is not enough to know the importance of a strong sense of self; we must also understand how to create it for ourselves. A later part of this chapter will focus on this aspect but firstly, let's discuss the factors that determine our perception of self.

Factors that influence **your sense of self**

Humans are not meant to exist in isolation. It is within our making, as social creatures, to live in the vicinity of others and have our sense of self shaped by these encounters. This factor of societal influence plays a preponderant role in shaping our perception of self. Whatever we perceive as defining our identity is altered by psychological and societal factors. A clear understanding of these factors will help clarify how a sense of self is initially formed, how our identities are shaped, and how we can begin to make conscious decisions that lead to adjusting and molding our self-image to reflect our core values as an authentic being.

Individuation

It was Carl Jung who coined the word individuation. The renowned psychologist defines individuation as "a slow, imperceptible process of psychic growth." Individuation is how you distinguish yourself from others. It is a type of growth that progressively brings about a more mature and developed personality. Essentially, it is the process through which a person forms a unique self, and it begins, like many things, during childhood.

Through the earlier years of our life, as we develop on various levels and interact with our environment, we can learn from our surroundings. We instinctively regulate our actions and reactions following the response from our environment. When we feel we are being heard and given room to express ourselves, we form a deep knowing that we are valuable and that our needs matter. We see ourselves as individuals who differ from others in terms of identities, behaviors, and ideas. More importantly, we are unshaken by knowing that this individuality can displease. We see our thoughts, views, and opinions as worthy of being held, within respect and understanding of the outside response. We don't doubt that our thoughts, feelings, and opinions are valid or worthy of being shared. We are well aware of and can define who we are and where we stand.

If we are not fortunate enough to grow up in a healthy environment promoting the above, our sense of individuality can turn out quite differently. An unhealthy environment that prevents us from speaking our thoughts greets our self-expression with criticism, judgment, or indifference, bringing about a weak sense of self. When our identities are not acknowledged, our feelings are ignored, our thoughts are neglected, and our ideas scorned, we may end up growing into adults who cannot see the value of their individual characteristics and beliefs.

If conditioned by an unhealthy environment to yield thoughts, needs, and wants and live according to others' standards, we may not see ourselves as complete individuals capable of communicating and affirming desires and ideas. As a result, our sense of identity can take a hit, often leading to a low sense of self.

Lacking a strong sense of self can result in depending on the feelings, opinions, and thoughts of others to lead their lives and make choices. Because they do not own up to their personal beliefs or views, they surrender (often before even trying) and become inadvertently guided by expectations and conventions. Other peoples' thoughts and opinions on what to buy, where to work, where to live, whom to choose as a spouse, and how to go about their life will continue to entrap them in a vicious cycle.

As the pattern of depending on others' opinions continues, you increasingly lose your sense of self, as you forget to reach out to yourself, first and foremost, to seek answers and guidance. This can easily lead to depression or anxiety and an overwhelming sense of hopelessness and helplessness. As individuation comes into play with building a strong sense of self, we become more aware and able to place ourselves in a position to conduct the affairs of our lives and be self-reliant. There is no doubt that happiness, freedom, and fulfillment can derive from having a strong sense of self.

Attachment

Simply put, attachment relates to how our early childhood relationships, especially with our parents, caregivers, or guardians, affect our understanding of other relationships later in life.

From very early stages, infants and toddlers will come to understand themselves within the parameters of their relationship with others. These first attachment patterns and interactions directly impact the evolving state of our emotional, cognitive, behavioral, social, and even physical health and development.

If secure and filled with unconditional love and acceptance, the attachment will bring about behavioral outcomes fashioned in a way that earns their approval. As we receive more and more affection and praise, we are conditioned to live our lives in alignment with what others expect from us and what fits their belief systems. Although mostly positive, this will unavoidably bring about a situation where we consciously or unconsciously suppress our own needs and desires and focus on granting those of our friends/family/spouse since we have been conditioned to believe that being agreeable is a way to show affection.

On the other hand, if the environment is toxic, your development can be hindered. It can leave a person thinking their entire life that their desires and needs are not valid. For example, fear of abandonment resulting from early childhood trauma can lead to an unhealthy or inexistent sense of self. It also creates insecure and emotionally reactive people who nurture a deep-seated belief that they are unlovable and inadequate. This will have a considerably negative impact on your identity development and how you handle your relationships later in life. You may find it difficult to fully accept and love yourself unless you intentionally work through the knots and free yourself from the grip of low self-worth.

The good news is that if consciously addressed and nurtured, these underlying obstacles to living with a definite sense of self can be moved to allow for healthy bonding, better relationships, as well as a more profound acceptance and understanding of others. This will bring about healthier, stronger, and more empathy-filled relationships.

Becoming a Social Chameleon

Part of the lizard family, chameleons, are famous for their ability to change colors to match their environment. With this ability, they can quickly transform to blend in, making it easier for them to evade capture and hunt their prey. Many of us employ these tactics when trying to fit into a social group or attempting to gain others' approval. Even though our veritable nature may contradict our actions and words, many of us are willing to sacrifice our core values, the essence of our being, to be part of something bigger.

Instead of having a firm hold on our sense of self, we are willing to alter our identity and beliefs to align with others. This is a trap. Eventually, a time will come when you will have been so degraded by these exchanges, by the lack of voicing opinions and making conscious choices, that recognizing or unearthing your true nature becomes very challenging.

An important factor that influences our sense of self is what we are willing to sacrifice to win social approval or conform to fit conventional norms. This factor is what I call becoming a social chameleon. In an attempt to fit into a social group, usually occurring in response to societal expectations, it is not rare for people to push their values and belief system aside. Agreeing to do things for lack of ability to say no is another symptom of this all-too-common problem. In itself, becoming a social chameleon will cause you to lose your authenticity, in a regretful betrayal of your inner truth. The need to please and the desire to fit in is a dangerous combination when it comes to factors that negatively affect our sense of self.

Self-worth and self-image are not something that we are born with; they must be carefully tended to and developed over time. For the sake of brevity, I will not embark upon the nature vs. nurture debate. However, various factors and influences, such as our environment and genetic predispositions, play a central role in determining how we develop our sense of self. We are all born with different temperamental tendencies, with which all external factors such as interactions and experiences with our environment become intertwined, forming our core self.

As we move along through life, our concept of self must continue to evolve and adapt. The more aware you become of your tendencies to blend in, thus dismissing your authenticity, the more chances you stand of avoiding falling into the trap of becoming a social chameleon.

The truth is that we can never be completely happy or fulfilled until we live our lives authentically, have the freedom to follow our hearts and embrace our instincts, and have confidence in being ourselves instead of following the crowd. Until you let go of who you believe you should be and give in to who you truly are, you will continue to struggle with your sense of self. To live a life of true freedom, happiness, and fulfillment, you have to live up to your values, care less about pleasing others, and focus on being the best version of yourself.

Building a strong sense of self

Now that we've covered the significance of having a strong sense of self and the different factors that play a role in influencing our self-image, we will focus on developing a strong sense of self that aligns with our potential, peculiarities, and personality.

You see, every journey to self-awareness and self-development begins with a conscious choice to do the work and face your truths. As the proverb goes, as long as there is a will to continue, there will be a way. Below are some key tips on how to build a lasting and robust sense of self. Wherever you find yourself on this path of self-discovery, you are sure to find one or more nuggets of wisdom to add to your self-development toolbox.

Diving Inwards

A more significant part of understanding who you are, accepting it, and committing to improving upon it is being courageous enough to dive inwards. It is to ask yourself those unpleasant questions that you have been avoiding, face memories or facts that you have been suppressing, and seek ways to be true to yourself.

This is the point when you chose to be unapologetically honest about the discrepancy between the current state of your life and what you truly want it to be. It is a time to define your priorities, needs, and desires in all aspects of your life. It is a time to decide to grow beyond who you thought you were meant to be and who you were conditioned to become. It is the time to summon your courage and forge a vision of what feels profoundly right – and to build your path towards achieving it.

At this point, I feel it is important to mention that all things in the world outside a person are merely a projection of one's perceptions. In this sense, we create our reality. Our thoughts shape our world and our life. Your reality is a direct reflection of all that you hold inside you. Hence, the more you learn to look inward, the more opportunities you will grasp as you uncover the power that you have. You will come to the realization that turning inward is the best means of drawing close to reality, one that is of your own conscious creation.

Turning inwards helps us achieve self-realization by altering the way we view our place in the world. As you learn to find comfort within yourself, your decisional power will get stronger, and you will come to embrace obstacles and fully own the directional control you hold on your life. As you settle into your authentic being, you will come to a place of understanding that your life does not have to be ruled by any external factors. This is excellent news. Diving inwards will make you the boss of yourself! No longer will anyone else be accountable for your successes, nor your mistakes. It is a package deal and one that comes with great rewards. You will see that you are so much more than what society has shaped you to be. There is so much inside you that you have yet to tap into.

Right on the inside is where truth resides as against all the noise, confusion, and lies that exist on the outside. Finding yourself is taking a front seat to your thoughts and witnessing all that has been holding you back. In all aspects of your life, the awareness behind the confusion will be revealed. Building self-image comes from looking inward; it is the only place where your true self can be found.

The Power of Affirmations

As you navigate towards gaining and strengthening a sense of self, knowing and having confidence in who you are, learning how and when to say "no," and learning to focus on caring for yourself, you will discover an array of tools at your disposition to support you along the process. I have come to use two highly useful and impactful tools daily: positive thinking and affirmations.

Every day, negative thoughts run through our heads. There is no avoiding this fact. However, depending on how we approach these thoughts, they might take up residence in our head or float on through. Allowing them to stay and dwelling on and nurturing them - can be very damaging to our psyche. Some valuable tools that can help us redirect or transform these unpleasant thoughts into neutral or positive ones are mindfulness, gratitude, visualization, and affirmation.

Positive affirmation, visualization, and gratitude have a way of altering our thought patterns. This process is very powerful and can even result in a complete alteration of our physiological responses. As we live in a fast-paced world that has us continuously stimulated by a flow of irrelevant stimulation, most of us come to deal with stress and feelings of anxiousness as a regular and permanent part of our life. Unless you live a highly-secluded lifestyle with little or no responsibilities, stress is an omnipresent aspect of everyday happenings. It is essential to understand the mind/psyche is intrinsically connected to the physical body, and changing one will impact the other, whether negatively or positively.

Positive thinking and mindfulness are conscious approaches to altering your thoughts. Yet, this can become an automated response with regular practice and eventually carve a path to the subconscious mind.

Daily affirmations help boost your confidence and make you feel like you can accomplish anything you set your mind to. There are plenty of recipes already created in this area, but you can easily make up some of your own as needed.

Affirmations are positive personal statements that promote self-empowerment and vary according to your individual needs. They should ultimately lead to a situation or goal that you would like to turn into reality. By repeatedly saying or visualizing these statements, we can change our perception of our environment and alter our mindset. It then becomes natural to detect the circumstances that will lead to your vision, and therefore instinctively seize an abundance of opportunities. You will soon find that your ideas have become your reality through a simple shift in mindset; a whole new world has now opened up to you.

There are some straightforward tips to help include visualization into your daily routine. Whatever your need, you will find there is an infinite number of affirmations at your disposal. For the purpose of our journey to self-discovery, the following propositions will help ground and center yourself and foster a balanced perspective of who you are. As most of us begin and end our day in bed, it is easy to include these statements at those precise moments. Here are a few examples of clear and concise and powerful statements:

- *I am ready for transformation.*
- *I welcome this emerging entity that is my essence.*
- *I am taking responsibility for my life.*
- *My sense of self is growing.*
- *I am open to a shift in energy in my life.*
- *I am grateful for the opportunities and life lessons that come my way.*
- *I invite authentic connections and abundance.*

As you will find in the accompanying workbook, there are numerous options readily available. However, the most powerful ones will undoubtedly come from yourself, as you picture your desired goals, habits, circumstances, and so trigger their realization.

I strongly advise that you carefully select statements that you can easily visualize. Affirmations and visualization go hand in hand and are powerful tools in discovering and embracing your true self.

Creating a Vision Board

Once you come to understand who you are and where you stand, you will be able to clearly define where you want to be. Your next step is to give wings to your plans. It is time to take action and challenge yourself to reach your goals. This is where a vision board comes into use. If you have begun to work with affirmations and visualization, this will come naturally into play. As a concrete tool to envision your life (present, short-term future, and long-term future), your vision board will mainly comprise details of the daily activities you must carry out to realize your goals.

So, what are vision boards? Simply put, they are a concrete visualization tool for realizing dreams, desires, and goals. This process usually involves finding or creating pictures and images representing your aspirations and collating information on a board. Doing this will enhance the visualization process, thus creating a more positive outlook on your life's potential. It will make you prone to attracting more of what you desire into your life by altering your mindset and propelling you to get to work to turn these dreams into reality.

Vision boards are inspirational and incredibly powerful in bringing to reality that which we desire and setting forth tangible ideas, dreams, and goals that you hold of yourself. Your vision board should be easily accessible and within sight during most of your day. This will allow your brain to fully process these goals and transfer them to your subconscious mind, where they will seed and flourish. Before you know it, you will realize how much your life has shifted without much of a conscious effort to do so.

Self in society

We live in the age of social media, TV, and high-level fashion, where we are constantly bombarded with images of what, who, and how we should be. Our environment is so polluted with negative and superficial information that even those with strong self-esteem can easily fall prey to these capitalist temptations, leading to a spurious life of people-pleasing instead of staying true to ourselves.

A strong and firmly rooted sense of self is key to leading a balanced life and highly beneficial to personal growth. It will allow us to go through life without being pulled right and left by the many external influences that seek to make us other than who we truly are. Armed with a solid sense of self, we can face adversity and come out stronger; we are able to live a life of value and self-fulfillment, achieving our goals and continue moving forward.

2

OWNING YOUR TRUTH

> "You either walk inside your story and own it, or you stand outside your story and hustle for your worthiness."
>
> — Brené Brown

It is in our nature to crave respect, dignity, and acceptance. In trying to achieve these things, we put ourselves in positions where what matters to us becomes secondary to what matters to others. Ignoring our feelings and emotions while seeking to gratify those of others becomes second nature.

We often mask how we feel inside because we're afraid of what others may say about it, or because we are fearful of being the recipient of their judgment, rejection, or unfair opinions, we hide away our feelings and desires and steer away from vulnerability.

What if we could live a life of authenticity, integrity, and honesty? What if we could live a life that is true to our values, principles, and inner wisdom instead of one based on others' opinions, expectations, or views? Now, understand that owning your truth isn't about "fixing" yourself. No one is broken; living life in itself is a work in progress. Our journey is unique and of substantial value. So, owning your truth is not about finding fault in who you are or the choices you have made. It is about stepping fully into the here and now. It's about owning the moment and choosing your own direction, almost as if you were the only existing being on Earth. Time to unshackle yourself from the prison of self-doubt and inadequacy. It's time to find your way to becoming the powerful, confident, and unique person that you are.

How can you become confident in yourself and not shy away from your truth? I will admit that it is a daunting process, one that will require you to step out of your comfort zone continually. Just as overcoming any fear, owning who you are to the fullest necessitates acknowledging that you have not been living authentically. Oh, the lies we tell ourselves! It is fascinating how we manipulate our thoughts to avoid tricky situations or make ourselves feel better. Single. Day.

But is it possible to remove the gap that exists between who you project to the world and who you truly are? Well, as is said, there is no more sure way to fail than never to try. Let's dive into the concept of owning your truth, and you may just find what you seek.

Emotional Intelligence

One essential ingredient for living a life of success, happiness, purpose, and fulfillment is emotional intelligence.

Some psychologists will argue that one's emotional quotient can be more impactful in determining success in life than the intelligence quotient. Some of the components of emotional intelligence are self-discipline, self-regulation, social skills, motivation, empathy, and this other factor that just happens to be our main area of interest: self-awareness.

There is no doubt about it: every individual is different, to some variable extent. We have different personalities and possess different needs, wants, and desires, with endless ways of expressing them. To successfully navigate these various aspects and correctly express them takes a certain level of cleverness and tact, one that does not necessarily fit the mold of intellectualism; in fact, it may well escape the understanding of those who experience life with a firm hold on rationalism. That is the wonder of emotional intelligence.

These different aspects of our lives are affected by certain factors, and so are expressed differently depending on what these factors are and how we respond to them. When you are emotionally intelligent, you know what you are feeling, understand what these feelings are telling you, see how these feelings affect others, and figure out how to express them correctly. Emotional intelligence is far beyond understanding your own emotions; it also involves perceiving and appropriately translating those of others.

As mentioned earlier, emotional intelligence is shaped by critical areas of personal and interpersonal skills or competence. Self-awareness is one of these factors and may even be described as the foundation on which all others are built.

Self-awareness

What is self-awareness? According to Daniel Goleman, self-awareness refers to the ability to understand your own emotions and their effects on how you interact with your environment. A self-aware person is not only capable of understanding their emotional responses as they happen but are primarily (and more difficultly) able to witness them from an outside observer's viewpoint. This is a powerful and challenging feat, as we are innately programmed to respond to and from emotions. Watching and monitoring how they evolve becomes a key to self-regulation, which helps maintain a focused and clear mind, untainted by extrinsic triggers and perceptions. You will see your emotions as an automated reaction and thus have a stronger hold on the extent of the emotional response to any given situation.

Apart from being aware of and making sense of your emotions, self-awareness also allows you to express more empathy as your understanding of your environment grows. Grounding into yourself, you will not feel the need to raise defensive shields and protect yourself from your environment. Sure, it will leave you susceptible to pain and quite vulnerable, but as you will soon discover, this is a crucial state of reaping the benefits of growing into yourself.

Emotional self-regulation

Mindful recognition of your reactions and emotional patterns is an essential step in the right direction, but it is a whole other challenge to express them adequately. This is where self-regulation, which we can also call self-management, comes in. As we move forward in this process and develop a better understanding of our emotional responses, self-regulation, a process by which you manage and adjust to environmental stimuli, naturally pieces itself into the puzzle. This creates a direct connection to learning how to manage or regulate your emotions properly.

Overreacting is an example of failure to self-regulate. Reframing negative thoughts is vital to having a clear outlook on your outside world, leading the way back into your true self. Life experiences can be confronting and testing. However, it is always within your ability, first and foremost, to modify your response to any given situation by conscious choice. I find it fascinating how much of our power evades us. As most of us grow up in a society defined by strict expectations, rules, and guidelines, we often forget the extent of our innate abilities and come to reduce our decisive power in making our life our own. This can lead to emotions being expressed in an unhealthy way, or at least one that does not serve us.

IMPROVING your self-regulation skills and living your life with dignity go hand in hand. This means that as you embark on this journey towards growing into your authentic self, you will work simultaneously on your ability to identify and mindfully manage stress triggers and find tools to center and ground yourself.

BEYOND ALL, let's not forget to nurture our feelings and emotional responses, as they are essential responses to lead us into wellbeing. Through daily habit management and observing our thought patterns, we can tame these instinctive and wild emotional reactions, living our lives one step ahead of them. I assure you that this is massive progress towards living authentically, as you will no longer be a victim of your brain's chemical reactions to stress. Adversity and challenges can become your allies when you understand the angle from which to greet them.

. . .

Discarding victimization

Studies have shown that one of the most significant factors affecting mental health is what psychologists call "internal locus of control," mainly taking responsibility for anything and everything that happens to you. It is a belief that you have control over what happens in your life and that you are not a slave or a victim of outside influence or power.

A healthy sense of control is a product of being able to firmly say "no" without feeling sad or guilty, exercising the right to set your own priorities, protecting yourself from harm, getting what you pay for (we don't always get what we think we deserve, and such is life), choosing healthy relationships, and creating your happiness in life. Not happy with something? Change it. Once you stop making excuses and come to take full responsibility for your circumstances, you will gain a sense of executive power and feel more centered.

Empathy

If you must genuinely own your truth, it is not enough to understand your own emotions or how best to express them; you also need to learn to understand others' feelings and be prepared to adapt to them. It is important to respect other people's right to own their truth and sentiment that comes from a place of empathy. Empathy is the capacity to see things from others' perspectives; to put yourself in their shoes.

Unfortunately, as a general rule that I was reminded of throughout my childhood, one cannot give what one does not have. This means that if you do not feel love towards yourself, it is highly improbable that you will be caring and openly loving towards others. Now, you are not condemned to carry this burden for all of your lifetime. As soon as you begin to alter how you perceive yourself and allow yourself to be perfectly flawed - a masterpiece of work-in-progress, I like to say – you will notice how finding beauty in everyone, and everything becomes so much easier.

Everyone is entitled to their own opinions and ideas. I am not saying you must accept certain behaviors, nor does it mean you should validate, condone, or sympathize with what others say and think. Remember, ideas are mere perceptions of a shared reality. Imagine observing cloud formations on a summer's day; one person may spot a dragon-like cluster, while the other can only find a flower-shaped cloud. Perhaps a third person sees nothing at all. This shows how one person's truth does not validate, nor does it invalidate another's.

Another thought on empathy: it is not always necessary to feel pain to understand it. Sure, you will be better equipped to relate to someone's feelings if you have been through a similar situation. But then again, we do not all react the same way to one given set of circumstances. So many factors come into play; it would be pretentious to assume that everyone feels and responds equally. One remarkably common misconception is how we assume that everyone thinks the way we do. But we'll dive further into that later.

Finally, empathy is a significantly important interpersonal skill that helps us interact and connect with others. With this skill, we can communicate better and build stronger, healthier, and more meaningful relationships. It is beneficial for those around you and incredibly helpful in your path to self-love.

. . .

Knowing your truth: personal value systems

As a focal point of this journey, knowing your truth makes an appearance on many levels of self-development. This is because failure to define the parameters of your life can have dangerous consequences. It can lead to a complete loss of your sense of self, impacting life-goals and ambition, relationships, mental health, and overall wellbeing. To embrace a life that is truly yours involves going through a process. I cannot hide that your findings may be confronting, and your truth may first exasperate you before it sets you free.

Finding your truth implies knowing who you are, what you want, and what you stand for. It entails understanding the actions and behaviors you must put forward to become whole. Standing firmly behind your values means not feeling the need to justify your actions and decisions. It means being unapologetically you.

By now, you understand how focusing on what other people expect of us and repressing who we are only to accommodate others' needs can lead to the loss of sense of self. Consistently repressing emotions, impulses, wants, and needs that reveal our true self has devastating effects on so many levels. The truth is, knowing who you are involves accepting how you feel and connecting with your deepest values. Betraying your values is equivalent to betraying yourself. Defining a clear set of personal values or a value system is a central component of the foundation upon which you grow as a person. It will affect all aspects of your life and clarify what you expect of others and, most importantly, yourself - in any given situation. There is no other way around it.

If you truly want a fulfilling life, you have to start by understanding who you are. As you pause to reflect on your path so far, you may want to put pen to paper (or keyboard to screen, whatever floats your boat) and ponder what truly matters to you. What are you willing to accept in different areas of your life, and where will you draw the line? This means tackling career, relationships, physical and mental health, and all other vital aspects of your existence. It means knowing what your nature and core essence are, what makes you tick, and what gives you a sense of fulfillment and self-worth. Nothing can be of more service to yourself than knowing where you stand and who you are.

SPEAKING **your truth**

Oh, the challenge. When did it become so difficult, so daunting, to come out and act like yourself? How did it become such a challenge to be proudly opinionated and debate one's point of view, passionately and respectfully? Knowing your truth is one thing, voicing it is another. When you chose to live authentically, your actions and words are naturally in alignment. This is a direct consequence of your clearly defined value system and promotes a healthy and well-rounded lifestyle.

Speaking your truth applies to all areas of your life. There is a certain level of power and freedom that comes with being able to speak your truth. It's not necessarily about challenging people or getting in their faces (even though I will admit that it sometimes may be quite tempting) but rather about self-affirmation. The time has come to lay down the law, and you have my utmost blessing to do so within your value system. Set down your boundaries, and abide by your decision to embrace who you are and what you believe to be right. You may not always be right; in fact, mistakes are a welcome personal growth factor. Oh well, you live and learn. Be kind to others, and before all, be kind to yourself. We are all a work in progress.

Opinions always have and always will differ. There is nothing wrong with a healthy expression of one's thoughts, within the knowledge that they are perceptions, not facts. Let's move to a space of compassion, where we allow ourselves to evolve at our own rhythm as we dance to our own beat.

Our truth runs deeper than any opinion, for it is about how we feel and all that matters a great deal to us. Speaking your truth isn't about being right; it is about expressing your mind in a transparent, authentic, and vulnerable manner and allowing yourself to be heard. It is about self-respect.

Being unapologetically **authentic**

We live in a society where we are always expected to follow the crowd, adhere to popular opinions, seek to please others, and value others' views. Would it be wrong to believe that these expectations can hinder our wellbeing? It may be how we've been programmed to act, but certainly not how we were meant to live. The truth is that we are free to be our own person, free to love ourselves for who we are, and free to be unapologetically authentic. As we are not programmed to think this way, it is a process of self-development to undertake. Just like speaking your truth, being unapologetically authentic is a choice to express yourself as a whole and unique individual.

The most genuine ways to experience living authentically are numerous. Refusing to apologize for having opinions and for experiencing emotions is a great place to start. There is also much to be said about belittling yourself, which has unfortunately become a synonym for humility. It is an absolute shame to witness people full of untapped potential knock themselves down to avoid impeding others' egos. This is often done to gain acceptance and to avoid confrontation and is an absolute barrier to self-development. If you can find the strength to be unapologetic, authentic, and wholehearted in the way you go about your life, you are more likely to experience fulfillment and happiness.

According to Brené Brown, an absolute legend in this field, being authentic is about making our own choices; the choice of being honest, and the choice to let the world see our true selves. Until you have learned to value yourself, you cannot ask others to respect and appreciate you. Let me emphasize that this does not necessarily mean putting others before yourself. It is a balanced approach to a healthy lifestyle. Until you pinpoint the things that are holding you back and make an effort to clear them out, you cannot truly be yourself. Until you you're bold enough to refuse to give in to the self-limiting factors of self-doubt, shame, and fear, you will never live to the level of your true potential. The decision is yours to make.

Understand that you have every right to refuse to be held down by popular opinions and societal expectations. You are allowed to reject the social paradigm which dictates when and how to appeal to others. Instead, choose to focus on what you want. Be concerned about being happy and fulfilled, and have no doubt that this will spread, for joy is highly contagious. Focus on things that put a smile on your face, and bring peace to your being. You are allowed to do away with anything that forces you to hide behind anyone's shadow or to make yourself less than you are.

Live fully. Be free, grasp every magical moment, and land into yourself. Let your authenticity be known. I encourage you to build your inner-strength and to solidify that unshakeable confidence that inhabits you. Connect to the most real and most profound part of who you are so that you can better understand what you came to this life to do. When you can make this deep connection and embrace the resultant discovery, you will no longer be bound by the need to be accepted by others. When you achieve this, nothing can stop you.

Our journeys are unique. No one else will get to experience what it's like to be you. You are in the most privileged position; embrace your power, and find peace in knowing that you were always intended to be none other than yourself.

HAVING the courage to be vulnerable

Imagine, for a moment, that the law firm where you work has just given you the nod to represent your first client in court. You did your very best to prepare for the case, but when the first court day comes, you see the legal team's quality representing the other party. You suddenly become nervous and fidgety, hands trembling, heart rate increasing, palms sweating. You become overwhelmed with certainty that your hard work won't pay off, that you will look foolish, and that you will struggle with making your case.

This experience highlights a situation of vulnerability, one that is not uncommon in our fast-paced, productivity-centered existences. These situations lead our body and mind to respond by resisting confrontation or avoiding the challenge because, let's be honest: no one enjoys public humiliation. Often consumed by our ego, we succumb to the temptation that is avoidance. However, avoiding confrontation, avoiding vulnerability does not build resilience. It does not make us stronger and certainly does not favor our path to self-reliance and acceptance. All those progress-hindering thoughts such as You'd *better turn around and go back home; You are not ready for this; If you speak, you will make a fool of yourself; what if you fail and people mock you,* come from a place of vulnerability. By pushing yourself to go through with the process, even with the possibility of being judged, mocked, or ridiculed, you are allowing yourself to experience something not only transformative but also healthy. In the words of Brené Brown, "vulnerability is the core, the heart, the center of meaningful human experiences."

After spending many years studying vulnerability, Dr. Brown came to this beautiful conclusion: "What scares us is sometimes actually good for us, and if we can stomach sitting with it, vulnerability has the potential to transform itself into joy." Vulnerability is what we experience when we are bold enough to step out of our comfort zone. It is a feeling that permeates our being when we attempt something that challenges us. It is the ability and willingness to entertain the emotional uncertainty of being right or wrong.

While putting ourselves in situations of vulnerability may be seen as a sign of weakness, that is not actually the case. The truth is that it takes an infinite amount of courage to accept to be vulnerable, whether it is exposing our truth within personal relationships, admitting when we are in the wrong and asking for forgiveness, opening up to others, or taking on new career challenges. As an automatic protection mechanism, we all possess a strong urge to avoid situations that make us emotionally exposed and vulnerable. Nevertheless, we must understand that this vulnerability is the foundation for creating many of our heart's desires, including self-fulfillment. It is when we put ourselves in a position of vulnerability that we can fully (and authentically) experience joy, courage, love, creativity, a sense of belonging, and empathy.

While stepping out into that courtroom to represent your client may make you very uncomfortable, it offers you a golden opportunity to expand and lean into your discomfort. It holds the potential to lead you into discovering new things about yourself, to grow personally and professionally, and develop new habits. A valiant First Lady once said: "No one can make you feel inferior without your consent." The power to take what you will from any situation is within your hands. Embracing a space of vulnerability can be life-altering and incredibly empowering.

YOU ARE ENOUGH. Let me repeat: You. Are. Enough. So, put yourself out there. Let yourself be seen, find the courage to be authentic, and let the world see the real you. Don't shy away from vulnerability, but rather embrace it. Being vulnerable is something to be proud of, for it shows that you are alive and willing to evolve and become a better person.

ALIGNING **with your SELF**

In a world led by ego where people are always competing and looking for ways to outdo one another, it is easy to become caught up in competitiveness and learn to think little of ourselves. When we find no other way to measure success than by mirroring our lives to others, we fail to see the beauty in what we accomplish. For optimal happiness and fulfillment, it is primordial to stay true to oneself; to align our thoughts and actions with all facets of our being. You will find that no matter how many times the world leads you astray, the best version of yourself lies within you.

> *"Knowing others is intelligence; knowing yourself is true wisdom. Mastering others is strength; mastering yourself is true power."*
>
> — Tao Te Ching

Aligning with ourselves is not a difficult thing to do, but often we get in the way of our true expression by suffocating who we are in an attempt to please others or conform to societal norms. We give in on things we should not compromise because we are afraid. We allow outside influences to dictate the parameters of our being and our existence. When we live like this, things that would naturally come to us are lost in the process of trying so hard to fit in.

The truth is, there is and will always be an infinite amount of ways in which to better ourselves. Perfection is an illusion, so why sacrifice unique parts of your making to fit a different mold? Forget inadequacy, incompleteness, and unworthiness. We are all born complete, with a fully-equipped toolbox; the time has come to learn how to use these tools.

On a final note, there are several ways in which you can learn to release old energies, fear-induced toxic patterns, long-ingrained insecurities fuelled by out-dated beliefs, self-destructive thoughts, and harmful attachments. Speaking to a therapist or a mental health specialist is often a catalyst to diving into yourself and re-aligning with who you are. Seeking help to better oneself is a powerful act of strength and courage.

ESTABLISHING **boundaries**

Once you've been able to get a grip on outside influences and have begun the process of defining your values, the next step would be to seek ways in which to establish where you stand and determine what you are willing to let in. As you learn to take responsibility for your thoughts and actions and their outcomes, setting emotional and social boundaries becomes vital in cultivating your sense of self in relation to others. They support you in gaining a sense of control over your actions, feelings, and physical space. Boundaries should reflect the outcome of a deep-seated personal value system. They dictate what you accept into your life and what you chose to dismiss for lack of service to yourself.

To create proper boundaries, you need to know as much as you can about yourself. That means knowing what is of high importance to you and pinpointing things that do not serve you. It is defining what is negotiable and what is not acceptable. Going through this process will allow you to get in touch with your emotions, beliefs, ideas, and feelings and teach you to sit comfortably with them. This developed inner intimacy helps you correctly measure the things you can and cannot accommodate, in other words, where you draw the line.

No one can know you better than you know yourself. This simple fact puts you in the best position to lead this journey. As you navigate the waters of growing into yourself, you will come to build self-reliance and hold yourself accountable for all your actions. Within your boundaries, people will come to understand what to expect, thus creating a natural process of eliminating the unwanted. As you begin to clearly state what is permitted within your space, all of which no longer serves your purpose will come to diverge into inexistence.

OWN YOUR TRUTH. Your experiences, mistakes, successes, and failures define not only who you are but also shape who you become, so don't be afraid to greet the package deal with open arms. You cannot expect to be held in high esteem if your self-respect is not established through principled goals and values and defined by clear boundaries. Work your way inwards, towards a place of acceptance. Welcome your flaws as a part of the whole unique entity that is your being.

3

LISTENING TO YOUR SOUL

> "As I began to love myself, I recognized that my mind can disturb me and it can make me sick. But as I connected it to my heart, my mind became a valuable ally. Today I call this connection WISDOM OF THE HEART"
>
> — Charlie Chaplin

Human beings are more than just muscles, bones, and blood. We possess a non-physical omnipresent component, one that most of us know little about. This aspect of the individual is known as the soul. The soul is, in part, responsible for the intricate workings of the mind and designated personality attributes. It is made up of mental abilities such as reason, character, consciousness, feeling, memory, thinking, perception, etc. The workings of the soul can be complicated and abstract. Most importantly, the soul is an aspect of the human make-up, which is the seat of our intuition, the inner self.

The soul has its own voice and is ever speaking to us through various means like feelings, sensations, and thoughts. We all have the power to receive this intuitive guidance from our inside but certain factors like overpowering emotional responses, stress, strong beliefs, etc. have a way of distorting the download of this information or message.

Unfortunately, the experience most of us have here on Earth has created a distancing with something that was once familiar to us at a soul level. Our life path and the lessons we encounter, if interpreted as such, can be viewed as an attempt to drive us back to what needs to make us true to ourselves and allow us to reconnect to our inner selves.

It is not easy to listen to and make sense of the messages being processed continuously through our system and demanding our inner self's attention. However, there are some tools and exercises at our disposal that can allow for a smooth download of information from our inner self so that we may claim back our power with an authentic twist.

Accessing your higher-self

Many of us have been in situations where we just know things even before obtaining tangible evidence of these happenings. Cases such as the betrayal of a loved one often seem to bring their lot of forewarning signs, whether we acknowledge their worth or dismiss them for fear of uncovering the truth. They are often unexplainable. It may be difficult to persuade others – let alone ourselves – that these signs are valid, as we often lack tangible evidence to support our convictions and claims.

Varying according to personal beliefs, intuitive hunches may be explained in many ways. About ten years ago, I recall a day when I first heard that clear yet subtle voice in my head. I was dating this man I had known for a short period. We were walking down a riverbank on a warm, sunny summer's day. It was romantic and comfortable, and I felt quite content. Yet somehow, out of nowhere, this voice echoed through my mind: "*Run.* Run away *now*." Now, I can assure you that this was not a motivational slogan to incite me to take on a fitness regimen (I was actually quite fit at that point in time); however, this clear, loud voice turned out to be an accurate signal. That relationship was doomed to fail, and when I think back on it now, I feel quite lucky that it ended early rather than later. Perhaps it was my higher-self, maybe my intuition. Spiritually speaking, some may be convinced beyond doubt that spirit guides were protecting me. Whichever option appeals most to you, we must reach the consensus that there is a wiser, higher guidance than our conscious way of living within society permits us to see. Let's take a further look into the concept of listening to your soul.

WHAT EXACTLY IS this concept of higher self? Well, simply put, it is the *real* you. It is an intrinsic part of your make-up and is ever communicating with you. It oversees your life and can grasp things that are not within your reach, as it is fundamentally unbiased and non-judgmental. Your higher self can process things you cannot grasp, for the physical body does not limit it within the restricted space of your tangible reality. It is a part of you that you can tame and learn to connect in order to expand your consciousness and gain a different perspective. When we say "only you know what's best," your higher self is, in fact, the all-knowing genius. Tapping into your higher self can guide and heal you in so many ways. It is the part of us that is wise beyond measure and unaffected by the sequence of positive or negative happenings in our lives.

The higher self is linked to innate wisdom and creativity and is not a product of our conscious mind. Think of all the dormant potential that lies within you. How beautiful would it be if we could tap into such unique insights? The truth is, we can and we will.

How can we access this higher self and increase the frequency in which we connect to it? As we've said, it is a part of us that is ever communicating. Still, we have become so accustomed to perceiving and experiencing through our physical senses that we've come to ignore this fundamental non-physical part of us. There are several ways through which we can connect with our higher self. Most of these methods are easily accessible, such as meditation (observing and detaching from thoughts), mindfulness (or mindlessness, if you prefer), exercise and play, creative expression, acknowledging your instincts, and harnessing your talents and gifts.

How to communicate **with your higher self**

The higher self is ever communicating, and it does so through various means such as dreams, gut feelings, intuitive hunches, and insights. We are continually connected to this source; our role is to be sensitive enough to pick up inner cues to lead us towards the best path to benefit our growth and development. These signals can be in the form of a funny feeling in the pit of your stomach, sweaty palms, or an unexplainable certainty that something is not as it should be. Let's look at some of the ways our higher self is communicating with us.

Gut Feeling

This is also known as gut instinct or intuition. It is a visceral knowing, beyond all reason and tangible evidence. You just know that something isn't right, even though you can't explain it. This knowledge is not derived from a conscious level but rather an intuitive one. Perhaps the entrance of a person into a room can cause you to sense a certain unusual energy; at times, you may feel a flow of positive energy upon meeting a person. Other times it may express itself as palpable tension in the air. We can sense these things as our instinct kicks in, even before our conscious mental faculties can make sense of them.

This gut instinct comes up as a feeling from within you, and only you can experience it. Since this feeling is personal, only you can tell how it feels, and conclude with your own interpretation. This is why only you can decide to listen to and follow your intuition. Acknowledging your gut feeling is a sign of trusting yourself.

Try picturing this. You've recently gone through a difficult break-up and separation from your (now ex) spouse. The end of the relationship was tumultuous. It has been a long and painful process, but you are finally beginning to feel free from the hold of your ex's toxic grip.

One day, you are feeling unwell at work. Deciding to head home to catch up on some much-needed rest, you arrive at your house earlier than usual that afternoon. As you pull into the driveway, you get a strange feeling of unease. You look around, but everything looks normal; you assume everything is normal and head for the front door. Finding your keys at the bottom of your work bag, you unlock the door and step into the house. The familiar space is welcoming; however, an uneasy feeling consumes you, reaching the pit of your stomach and squeezing into your chest. It is difficult to pinpoint, but as you turn around and notice the open window that you had shut before going to work, the familiar odor in the air brings clarity. At once, the image of your ex fills your mind's eye, and understanding sets in: you know, without a doubt, that he is in the house.

This scenario is not uncommon, and it is one example that shows how our instincts can help process all that happens around us. Whether or not you are an observant person, it is impossible to grasp every detail, every happening in our daily surroundings. However, we have a way of taking in information on a subconscious level. Sometimes it manifests itself emotionally or physically, at times without being able to identify the source consciously. We know, but we don't understand how or why. Our subconscious mind, which is also the source of dreams and storage of unresolved issues, influences our thoughts and feelings and ensures that we respond to our environment as per our programmed self.

Whatever you deduced regarding the origin of the odor in the house, it was an obvious trigger to previously suppressed thoughts – in this case, the unpleasantness of a painful separation – and might have been the residue of your ex's perfume floating in the air. Perhaps there was an extra pair of shoes in the hallway, one that you hadn't consciously taken notice of, but that your brain had associated with memories of a shared life, creating an emotional reaction.

Charlie Chaplin once said: "As I began to love myself, I found that anguish and emotional suffering are only warning signs that I am living against my own truth." Bearing this in mind, we can now make a connection between gut instinct or intuition and living authentically. Authenticity is vital, and it is a powerful game-changer. If listened to and nurtured, intuition and instinct can be enhanced and reveal many inner-truths, intensifying our daily life experience.

Intuitive hunches

Intuitive hunches occur when you feel subtle nudges to do or say something. We all have experienced these inner cues to visit a particular place, stay at home, attend an event, meet someone, or avoid a person. These nudges are ways through which your higher self communicates and guides you to a better path.

Now, I will say this: the higher self is always right. It is meant to be a guide, and it is competently doing that job. The only problem comes from the place of downloading the information and transferring it to the mind. This information, whether received as an intuition, dream, insight, or a hunch, in its purest form, can be interpreted in a number of ways. Although it is an untainted part of your awareness at the source, it can become diluted with your emotions and thoughts and distorted into misinterpretation. However, with practice, you can improve your mode of access and quality of download of this information. Developing your ability to focus and clear your mind, observing your environment, and responding unbiasedly, improving impartial thought-observation through practices like meditation, mindfulness can be highly beneficial in connecting to your essence. Additionally, learning to identify and separate wishful thinking from real gut feeling or insights is a fundamental part of the process.

. . .

Thoughts vs. reality

As the common iceberg analogy goes, our mind operates in ways that allow merely a glimpse of what is at the surface of its workings. There is so much more hidden out of sight: countless concepts beyond our reach and notions we cannot grasp. Our thoughts float about, in and out of the surface of our mind, and are mere representations of every component of our existence. Thoughts are affected by several factors, such as emotions, upbringing, personal beliefs, and much more. Just as the top level of the iceberg, perhaps 10% of its entire composition, is apparent above sea level, your conscious thoughts are only a minor part of the workings of your mind. There is so much information that we take in without processing, and most of what does appear in our train of thoughts does not particularly serve us.

With the practice of mindfulness and meditation, you can come to patiently observe your thoughts as they make their way through, witnessing them from an unbiased and non-judgmental perspective. In a world where we are continually overstimulated, overburdened, and under constant pressure, this process can decrease unnecessary information upload that often generates emotional responses. This process takes time and regular practice; it is a habit to develop for long-term benefits. Most of us are not conditioned to be observers of our thoughts; instead, we are taught to respond to our environment by immediate reactions and raising shields driven by one's ego. Staying in tune with your thought patterns can eventually alter your protective mechanisms and help you go through life with a much lighter load on your shoulders.

At this point, you might want to take a moment to pause.

Close your eyes if you need to. Take a few deep breaths. At this point, can you differentiate your perceptions from the actual, factual circumstances to which you are prone to react? You may want to look back on the last 24 to 48 hours of your life. Everything you did, from grocery shopping to parking the car, from minding for loved-ones to answering emails, could have been a trigger. In fact, it often is. Many daily misinterpretations lead us to react negatively, which harms us more than we can imagine.

Your subconscious mind is processing every sensation and experience that goes through your mind every moment of the day – this being the 90% of the iceberg underwater. Everything that you've experienced since the day you were born is kept in this enormous vault. This reservoir will continue to receive and store experiences until your last breath. By taking action and altering your conscious thought patterns, you are filtering the quality of information that will be stored subconsciously, as your subconscious responds to your already established behavioral patterns.

Only a fraction of your experiences and knowledge can be accessed while the rest are hidden away in your subconscious mind. When you experience emotional reactivity episodes with physical symptoms such as sweaty palms, an uneasy feeling, or knowing something before actually knowing it, your intuition is trying to download information from your subconscious into your conscious mind. Your subconscious accesses the stored knowledge and experiences and uses them to help you make sense of situations to preserve or keep you safe. It works on autopilot, mostly helping you view and interpret reality through the way in which you were conditioned.

On the other hand, your thoughts come from your conscious mind and are not real, but only your interpretation of reality. The truth is, even if you spend all your time thinking about something, it will not alter what it is. Stressing about a job interview and overthinking all that could go wrong will not change the outcome. All the energy you've put into focusing on fabulation sacrifices clarity, focus, and productivity.

Your thoughts are not your actual reality. They are and always will be a representation, and therefore it is within your power to alter their impact on your body and emotional responses. Sitting in silence, even for five minutes every day, and observing the flow of your imagination, may be a very impactful method to gain more connection to your thought patterns and to yourself.

PRIORITIZING **self-respect**

Standing your ground and refusing to follow the crowd can be extremely daunting. It leaves us in a highly vulnerable state, as it is part of our making to seek acceptance and belonging. When we have spent a large chunk of our lives people-pleasing, it can be quite challenging to speak freely and act as we please.

Knowing your priorities and respecting your individuality can be a challenging concept to implement, as you might struggle with not seeking outside validation and gratification. Establishing clear-cut boundaries through knowing your values and priorities can help make sense of where you stand and where you should draw the line. This will allow you to focus on what matters most to you.

Doing all these things can only happen once you have clearly defined what is most important to you. When you do, it becomes easier to respect your needs and wants and speak your mind, rather than ignoring or suppressing them. This is not only crucial for your sanity but can also impact your general health and wellbeing.

The capacity to make authentic and life-defining decisions is mainly dependent on what your priorities are. Priorities and personal values serve as a toolkit with which you can better understand yourself, and they are those upon which you rely to set healthy boundaries. As you learn to do this, it will lead to clarity about who you are, your values, and the best way to approach life.

What does knowing your priorities and respecting your wants and needs look like?

- It implies being honest enough to recognize what you most need and commit to acknowledging rather than dismissing them.
- It is being unapologetic and direct when it comes to making your priorities known to yourself and others. In other words: creating *boundaries*.
- It is knowing that having unique needs and wants is perfectly normal.
- It is being able to take responsibility for your actions.
- It is having a growth-mindset and expecting favorable outcomes.

Your values are one of the most essential factors in your life. They form the support structure of your life. Your values determine what you accept or reject as part of your existence. They define the choices you make, and these choices then determine the direction of your life. Our values should influence all of our decisions. Stick to your core values and listen to your heart.

Many of us disconnectedly navigate life, suppressing our innermost needs and desires. It is instilled in us from an early age to accept our carers' rules and values and our upbringing's social model. There comes a point in our lives when we must decide if we wish to continue down that path or step away from conventions and get to know our true selves. Until you define the rules by which you want to live and experience life, you are simply not living authentically. You are a prisoner of your shadow until you claim yourself back, taking hold of all that is truly important to you, values, and actions mirroring your soul and reflecting your heart.

At this point, the values transferred to you during your upbringing matter very little, nor does it matter which values are directing your current life choices. Understand that having clearly defined personal values is how you show respect to yourself. The only values that matter are the ones that can bring you happiness, meaning, fulfillment, connection and success in life are your core values, the non-negotiable ties to the deepest part of your heart and soul.

Take some time to determine what invigorates you, what makes you want to get out of bed every morning. I'm sure you've heard this before, but have you ever actually tried? Have you ever stopped to contemplate what may be your soul's calling, however accessible, possible, or out of reach it might seem to be? What is it that you would happily lose sleep over, what is it that you want to be remembered for? What brings an instant smile to your face and colors your life and that of others?

One other thing. Values are not written in stone; just as you are continually striving to become a more balanced person, your values are subject to change. What matters most is that these values which influence and guide your life come from you and are not what others determine is "right." As you evolve and grow through challenges and adversity, your values may need to be realigned, which is more than fine. Allow yourself to test the waters of existence, to improve, and strive to become a better person. Seize the moment, and grasp those opportunities. Don't let yourself be the one to stand in your way.

LASTLY, no one can dictate your path if you do not allow them to do so. Your truth is your identity, and no one can deny you this power unless you give it away. Know your priorities, define your boundaries while respecting those of others, and see yourself become a more authentic version of yourself.

RELEASE & connect through sharing

Life as we know it is not one linear line. It has its thrills, stresses, pains, and pleasures. It is full of influential factors such as work, family, politics, and societal expectations that can burden our emotional state, just as they can excite and thrill us. Added to them are the ever-increasing pressures of relationships, technology, beauty, and fashion (to name a few), all of which can leave us in a position of mental struggle.

When we are faced with these challenging situations, our actions and reactions are expressed in the form of emotions. These emotional responses can range from anger to shame, from fear to confusion, happiness, sadness, and loneliness, just to name a few. These emotions are powerful, and most are an overpowering part of our lives because they are how we view and interpret our reality.

Being a significant part of our everyday experience, emotions must be handled carefully and healthily, or we will fail to reap its attendant benefits. Feelings are normal and healthy, so they should not be ignored, suppressed, or treated with disdain. They are to be thoughtfully responded to and dealt with adequately. There are very healthy and efficient means of dealing with emotions, whether negative or positive. A productive way of doing this is through talk therapy.

Talk therapy, also known as psychotherapy or counselling, is founded on the basic idea of talking through emotions to put them into perspective. This approach is also useful in treating other issues such as depression, chronic stress, anxiety, etc. The primary goal of any therapy is helping patients to better deal with their life situations. This system, usually beginning with seeking out a professional therapist, provides a suitable means to connect with your emotions and release them.

As said above, there is always a better way to handle emotions other than ignoring, drowning, or suppressing them. Suppose the chosen method to deal with emotions fails to address the situation adequately. In that case, it will only lead to the perpetuation of whatever it is you're trying to avoid in the first place. Any method that is not the right way of dealing with these emotions can create suffering and prevent you from living fully. A reliable, time-tested means of dealing correctly with these emotions is through mindfulness.

As per Oxford Dictionary, mindfulness is defined as "a

mental state achieved by concentrating on the present moment, while calmly accepting the feelings and thoughts that come to you, used as a technique to help you relax." Mindfulness can be seen as a meditative state, through which you focus on paying attention to specific aspects of your surroundings or dive inwards and pay attention to your breathing. It may involve doing a body scan, which allows you to entirely drop into the present moment and notice how every single part of you is feeling. Perhaps if you stop and listen, you'll hear a bird chirping, or discover a faint smell of freshly mown grass, or even observe a cloud that looks surprisingly like your uncle Fred.

MINDFULNESS IS all about being present in the moment and tuning in with yourself. With short bouts of regular practice, it can turn negative emotions (anger, grief, anxiety, embarrassment, remorse) into a neutral emotional state. Transitioning into acceptance, these can become important sources of strength and wisdom. How is this possible? Regular mindfulness practices can alter how we view and react to these emotions. It is by turning towards these emotions, facing them, accepting them, and releasing them once they have served their purpose. As the wise Eckhart Tolle has said, "Whatever you fight, you strengthen, and what you resist, persists." It is crucial to our personal development to learn to lean into discomfort; "Trying to feel the feelings, staying mindful about numbing behaviors, trying to lean into the discomfort of hard emotions" (Brown, 2010). Dr. Brown goes on to add that "we cannot selectively numb emotions. When we numb the painful emotions, we also numb the positive emotions." If you can find the strength to feel your way through vulnerable experiences mindfully, you will discover a much deeper connection to your true self and build your strength of character and resilience.

MINDFULNESS ALLOWS FOR KIND, compassionate, caring, and patient attention to whatever you're going through. It is a means of regulating emotions and connecting to your authentic self. Below is a sequence of steps to help in dealing with challenging emotions mindfully. It is a process I learned as a young adult and have used it successfully many times over the years. In this technique, visualization is key.

1. **Noticing**

Noticing is the art of mindful observation. It is the initial state during which you feel the emotional response in your body, sometimes manifesting itself through tears, stomach pain, skin rashes, tightness in the chest, sweaty palms, and more. The first step to begin dealing with these emotions is to notice them. Pause for a moment, take a deep breath, sit with the guilt, shame, anger, fear, frustration, or anxiety, and observe them without judgment. Avoid inhibiting, ignoring, or suppressing these emotions. Simply notice and entertain them with an attitude of acceptance and open curiosity.

2. **Identifying**

After you've spent a moment observing your emotions, you should now identify what they are. You may wish to verbalize what the feelings are; this creates a sense of lightness and makes you consciously aware of what you feel. Begin with statements such as "I feel anger" or "I feel sadness," while visualizing the area in your body where you feel this emotion. You should avoid statements such as "I am angry," as they personify emotions. You are not your emotion, nor does it possess you. Using the former statements is powerful, as it allows simultaneous detachment and empowerment. You are permitting yourself to feel this way. It is a form of self-compassion and opens-up a gateway towards the next step.

3. Accepting

Imagine you are greeting a long-lost friend with open arms. That is precisely the way you should approach your emotional response. It serves you for a higher purpose; it is part of your making and a sign of vitality. Accepting your emotion implies feeding it love. I like to picture myself cradling the emotion as I would an infant. While this may sound strange, it is a potent tool in releasing negativity. When you are capable of embracing the parts of yourself that you would usually suppress, everything shifts. You are now feeding yourself pure, non-judgmental, untainted love. Acceptance is a significant step in the process of letting go.

4. Releasing

"To let go does not mean to get rid of. To let go means to let be. When we let be with compassion, things come and go on their own." (Kornfield, 2008)

After accepting your emotions and feeding them love, the next step is to let them go. At this point, you will have created a distance between yourself and these feelings, so all that is left to do is to release them.

To do so, I suggest you use another visualization technique. When you feel ready, as you hold your pain, you will choose to send it back out of yourself and direct it into the universe. This is one of many ways; it is a very personal process, and you must choose a method through which you feel comfortable. Like everything else, practice makes perfect. The more you practice visualizing, the easier it will become.

Now that we have covered this four-step process, you are better equipped to be mindfully accepting of your emotions. Go ahead and hold them in your awareness, sprinkling them with some much-needed TLC. This alone will help to soothe and calm you, as it is also a meditative process. Ultimately, it helps create somewhat of a mental space around emotional responses, making it possible for you to witness from a distance instead of struggling through a state of tumult.

As we function through a limited perspective of life and all that is possible, it is beyond our conscious ability to see the invisible. One of our largest and most impactful misconceptions is that we assume that all others think the way we do. As such, it has been said that no one sees what you see, even if they see it too. Sit with yourself and take notice of your inner-voice; connect to your soul. Can you reach outside this paradigm and listen to your higher self?

4

CONNECT WITH YOUR INNER CHILD

> "Each one of us has an inner child, or way of being. Getting in touch with your inner child can help foster well-being and bring lightness to life."
>
> — Dr Diana Raab

Before diving into this topic, let's go over the concept of the inner child. Your inner child is an innate aspect of yourself that paints the picture of the "little you." This metaphorical child is the source of all childhood memories. It is at once your innocence, the untainted and pure being that you once were, full of wonder and unhindered by societal barriers. This inner child experienced all of your earliest emotional traumas and comforts, as well as the numerous memories that came with them. Some still live at the surface of your mind; others, as a means of self-preservation, have been long-buried into your subconscious. Although they have yet to be resurrected, these experiences still significantly impact your everyday take on life. They come to shape our emotional responses and influence our decision-making process. It is clear to see why the inner child is the foundation of who we are today, the lens through which we perceive and respond to our world.

In the same way that a healthy child can be fun, playful, and resilient, a traumatized or injured child might develop a challenging adult life, particularly when his or her adult life experiences trigger the reappearance of buried past wounds.

Everyone has wounds. Bitter, painful, or unpleasant experiences often remain tied to our inner child. Whether we dare to admit it or not, the fact remains that our sensitive and vulnerable inner child yearns for love and approval. If it was not received then, we will still crave it now. Without healing, you will find yourself continually transferring those past wounds to your life today, most likely amplifying the consequences as you go. Whether the source of the emotional scars can be traced to psychological or physical abuse, a broken family, or the loss of a loved one, the resulting pain will be attached to us for all our lives; and we can be reminded of this anytime, anywhere. Traumatic experiences cannot be undone, but healing from these wounds is possible.

When we connect to our inner child, we can access information that will make us understand some of the frequent obstacles we face, such as negative patterns that impair our self-development and self-actualization. It is possible to uncover the unhealed wounds, what is responsible for them, and how we can heal those wounds, on a profound level, so that we can live in our world of today as well-rounded adults. This connection can bring about in-depth healing and lead to the transformation of our lives.

Below are some strategies that can help connect to your inner child so that you can heal and experience the best that life has to offer.

Forgive yourself

We may want to deny it, but the fact remains that our past stays with us. Dreams are a standard gateway for repressed memories or past events to resurface. Our past often finds a way to replay itself in our present, and in doing so, influence our future. The past is who you were, today is who you are, and tomorrow is who you will be. You must understand that all of these aspects are intrinsically connected; therefore, altering one will influence the others. Ask yourself this question: which of these is within your control? How can you change one aspect to shift the direction of your life?

Many of us have this firm belief that holding onto past mistakes is unfavorable. Yet, many of us repeat said mistakes because we do not know how to free ourselves from this vicious cycle. The thing is until you shift your perspective, you will continue to be held back by the hurt, pain, and negativity of yesterday. To start healing from past wounds and put yourself on the right path for the life of today, you must face your past head-on. Speaking to a specialist is often a powerful starting point. Sit in your discomfort, deal with our pain, heal your wounds. Treat them kindly and respectfully, for they are the foundation of your making. And you will *know* when you are ready to move forward. Your inner child will be free. You will move freely towards your future and back into your true self.

Yes, your upbringing might have been a less than perfect one, and your caregivers, parents, or guardians may have let you down on several grounds. But one thing you must come to terms with – and this will help you deal with the problem – is the fact that they are after all human, thus inevitably prone to mistakes. Remind yourself of this regularly to avoid empowering your past. If it is not beneficial to your self-development, what is done should be left behind you. Understand that blame doesn't help anyone, and it certainly does not serve you.

Obviously, merely being aware of this fact will not make your trauma or pain magically disappear. Yet, one of the things it will do for you is to prevent past wounds from festering. Holding on to the ugliness of your past for too long can lead you to the point where you harbor resentment, are held captive by your own pain and abide by a victim mentality.

This is when you should consider connecting to your inner child to help you correctly manage the situation. Doing so may give you insight and lead you to recognize that your emotions are possibly a derivation of your past challenges. We sometimes react from a childlike perspective when confronted with unresolved issues from our upbringing, these of which often result in emotional insecurities. Your inner child is ever-present, but he is not who you are today. You have the power to determine what should stay in your past and what belongs to your present and will serve you in the future.

I urge you to tackle unresolved issues headfirst and avoid

dwelling on your past: your upbringing, the circumstances of your childhood, your successes, and failures. Dwelling on what is done is like bathing in your filth, day after day; it is uncomfortable, messy, and offers no positive outcome. It is unhelpful and will hold you in the grip of longing and despair. Furthermore, it will serve you to no extent, merely hindering your ability to progress and move forward on your journey. Sure, it will take courage to remove yourself from the grasp of self-pity. Pull that plug and drain that tainted water; it is time to refill and cleanse. Believe me when I say this: the temporary discomfort of facing your past will be well worth the opportunities that await you on the other side.

Give yourself permission to be flawed

Cognitive distortions

The human brain is wired to control movement, sensations, and thoughts. I am not suggesting that we ignore or second guess what our brain tells us every time, but there are instances where second-guessing instinctive reactions may be of great benefit. Your brain may have developed some unhelpful connections over time. You will be surprised to discover how common it is to make non-existent connections between ideas and thoughts. This tendency of the brain to make faulty connections is the foundation of cognitive distortions.

So, what are cognitive distortions? Essentially, they are thought patterns that alter our perception of reality. Moreover, they are usually negatively biased. What does this mean? It implies that we often inhibit our potential by the means of automated negative thought patterns. It is one of our many coping mechanisms and is a common way of dealing with adversity.

Often unreasonable and illogical, these beliefs and thoughts unknowingly become reinforced over time. The thing about these types of thought patterns - and the reason we need to be aware of them - is that they are very subtle and difficult to recognize, even (especially) when they are a regular occurrence. Cognitive distortions come in different forms, such as emotional reasoning, overgeneralizing, filtering, jumping to conclusions, catastrophizing, etc. and have the following thing in common: they are inaccurate or false patterns of thinking that have the potential to cause psychological damage.

Many of us are quick to point out that we cannot be held down by distorted thoughts or fall prey to them, but the truth is, complete denial makes us even more vulnerable to these destructive beliefs. The goal is not to avoid these thought patterns at all costs but rather to acknowledge them and reflect on how they impact our lives.

Let me show you how easily we can get caught up in cognitive distortions.

We all view ourselves in a particular way, often projecting to the world a version of us that we want others to see in order to be accepted. Knowing that this image that we have created for ourselves makes us feel valued by people and puts us in a dignified position, we tend to keep it up, and even when this person we have created no longer exists, we pretend to stick to that personae.

As time goes by, extra layers are added to this image so

that our flawless appearance continues to be seen as perfect. This leads to a situation where we are unable to relate appropriately with people because we're afraid to let them see our flaws. Our private life may be a mess, and we may be unhappy because our life revolves around living up to the personae that we think others expect. Just like Jim Carrey's character in *The Mask*, you may slowly mold into the person you are projecting to others while neglecting your true self.

If we are not ready to accept the fact that we are not the perfect person we say or let people think we are, it becomes challenging to come to terms with our imperfections. In trying to defend our position, we may begin to blame our friends, the weather, fate, or our background for any perceived flaw instead of simply accepting the fact that it's okay not to be perfect. As a result, we harbor false and illogical beliefs, drawing conclusions where none exists and making irrational generalizations. Here are some examples of such cognitive distortions:

- *I must be perfect or seen to be perfect*
- *Some people are perfect*
- *It is a sign of weakness to accept that I am flawed or imperfect*
- *People will hate me if they find out I'm not perfect*
- *I am stupid, and that is why my partner left me*
- *I am the unluckiest person in the whole world*
- *I couldn't even do that; I'm never going to amount to much in life*

There are endless examples of cognitive distortions where people interpret their reality in inaccurate and often negative ways. They become overwhelmed by this flawed thought process and will begin to interpret circumstances through feelings.

There are many ways to go about undoing this kind of harmful thinking, the first one being to acknowledge those unhelpful thought patterns. As we've already discussed, talking to someone and sharing your concerns may help get things in motion. Repressed thoughts tend to resurface when we verbalize them. Also, coming to terms with the fact that you don't have to be perfect to live a happy, successful, and fulfilled life will allow for a truer, more authentic dialogue within yourself. Being flawed is part of human complexity (and who is to determine what should be considered a flaw, anyway?) and will not make you any less than you are. Welcome your weakness, as they are full of dormant potential. Being vulnerable has a way of drawing you closer to your true self. Allowing and embracing this perception will help you to deal with cognitive distortions effectively. It will give you permission to be you and the freedom to make mistakes, evolve, and grow. It is alright to be beautifully and perfectly flawed.

Break down

Have you ever been in a situation where you just hate your life? You step back and take a look at who you've become, or how you are living, and you can tell that something is missing? Maybe you just have this feeling that this life you're living isn't yours. This is because your existence has been forged on the grounds and influence of others. Perhaps you have been trying to conform to a set of rules, norms, and expectations, and in doing so, you've neglected your true self. It is a common trait in most societies to abide by certain codes. We have all been, to some level, socially, emotionally, and mentally conditioned to live by the rules of others, to respond to the expectations of parents, spouses, friends, and family. In this process, our self-expression was most-likely inhibited. The constant struggle between acceptance of others and creating our own path can be overwhelmingly challenging. As a result, it is easy to lose control of our life, to lose our sense of purpose, and ultimately have no idea who to be and how to live a life that is truly ours.

As a young child, you were undoubtedly free-spirited. You probably loved to visit the back of the house and play in the dirt; maybe you enjoyed talking to animals and creating fantasy worlds where you could stay for hours. You were infinitely curious and wanted to understand every single aspect of your environment.

In becoming the adult you are now, you most likely had to take apart the person you were many years ago. Social conventions and expectations tend to dictate how we progress through those teenage years, and as the habits solidify, they keep hold of us as we enter adulthood. We learn when to speak and when to be quiet. We are taught exactly how to act to gain others' approval, which is often perceived as a means to success. We may stop questioning for fear of being wrong or, worse, for holding absolute certainty that we have full knowledge of all there is.

As a direct result of your response to societal rules, how you express yourself is derived by how you perceive yourself within your environment and forms the foundation of who you are. Although there can be many barriers to self-expression, it is one of the ways in which you project your personality by sharing ideas and communicating thoughts. Self-expression is the way we express or make ourselves known.

There are many ways through which you can express your authentic self. It can take various forms, some of which are talking (verbal or non-verbal), facial expressions, body movements, actions, and physical appearance. When your manner of expression is interrupted, corrupted, or weakened by anyone in any way, it can set the tone for who you become for the rest of your life. Healthy self-expression is a vital part of your life and wellbeing. The journey of self-discovery can be seen by some cultures as selfish, unusual, odd. Unfortunately, it can even be perceived as a time-wasting endeavor, but the truth is that self-expression is of great importance in society. If no one speaks their mind and everyone acts the same, there is no room for change and evolution. In fact, "the journey of self-discovery is the most important journey we can take" (De la Huerta, 2014). Self-expression provides a platform for us to be ourselves, attain fulfillment, and contribute richly to our world.

Genuine and authentic self-expression is how we embrace who we are, whether it be the positive traits that we proudly expose or the dark and less valued parts that we are quick to hide away. Apart from the fact that true self-expression encourages us to be our best, it creates room for us to work more effectively with others (Glaser, 2016). Through self-expression, we can move away from our protection mechanisms and eventually begin to open up to others.

Many of us are stuck in his situation. We may be seen to be doing well, but the truth is that our life is full of fears, self-doubt, low self-esteem, and shame. It's time to breakdown these barriers; it's time to be truly YOU. Choose to reclaim passion for your life.

No one knows you better than you know yourself. No one but you can and should choose how you live your life. It's time to go back to who you were when it all started, to the place where you feel whole.

Perhaps the time has come to break down the multiple

layers of your fake façade, the one you have been cultivating since your first breath. Who was there before it all, before norms, rules, and expectations? What is the essence of your soul?

Unbury potential

In the late 1960s, NASA developed a series of tests regarding sources of creativity, innovation, and imaginative ability. They were hoping to discover whether these factors are inborn, learned, or acquired by experience. These extensive experiments led to the conclusion that it is not that children lose the ability to be creative, but that it is taught out of them. The data collected showed that our school system's education robs us of our innovative, creative, explorative, and imaginative genius.

As children, we were naturally curious about the world and always eager to know why things are the way they are. We loved to freely explore our environment, being instinctively intuitive and perceptive, and paying attention to the little things. These attributes and others are an essential part of what makes children highly innovative and creative. The traditional schooling system, teaching us how to behave in society, can come to repress many of these natural tendencies. School is, for the most part, a place of conformity. And although many educators try their best to allow kids to remain as they are, the school system does not concede enough space for individuals to strive for uniqueness. It has slowly and progressively erased them while dumbing down in the process.

According to researcher Judith Glaser, the state of our

inner child is where we are most innovative. She states that when we align with our true self, our inner self, a part of our brain known as the prefrontal cortex is activated, thereby granting us higher access to abilities such as innovative and creative thinking, planning, and problem-solving. This is one more reason why we should seek to reconnect with our inner child.

Take time to cultivate your inner child, get involved in things that will set your soul on fire, and by so doing, provide yourself with the needed opportunity to free yourself from any dumbing down that years of education and schooling has done on you. Tap into your inner child to create, invent, explore, and innovate. Give yourself the liberty to be your true self again.

Emergence

Think about this: What are the things that naturally make you laugh? What is a sure way to turn your frown upside down? What thoughts bring you tears of joy? What memories make your heart glow?

We all have some wonderful memories of when we were little. A time when we would endlessly jump on the bed, throw pillows, and cover our faces with our underwear, a time of pure, fresh, and renewed interaction with our surroundings. Those were moments of play, moments where we had no worries in our minds, moments of unlimited fun, and pure bliss.

So much has happened between then and now that we have forgotten about those moments of wild and unbridled laughter, smiles, and joy. The infinite demands of adulthood can subtly take over what used to be silliness and carelessness. Endless time-consuming demands keep us disconnected from our inner-child.

Some people are ever bothered by this change; it can be seen as the natural order of things, so they are not perturbed. Some believe childhood is the time to play, and when that time comes to pass, we must move on and focus on making the right choices and being responsible. The question is, have we truly outgrown our inner-child?

What if we were to hold on to some of the beloved aspects of our little selves and watch as they flourish into adulthood? You can try to recall what defined you as a person before becoming an adult or even before your teenage years. What soothed you, and what made you react? Who were your friends, and what kind of person did you enjoy spending time with? This is not to say that we must not evolve; all the opposite. We do often outgrow places and people. Such is life. However, if you can reach back to a time before all the societal grooming and conditioning, back to when you were unburdened by the worries of this world, you may tap into the innocence of your soul and your true essence.

Next time you are faced with an unpalatable situation, reconnect with your inner child; remember those things that naturally make you laugh and smile; those thoughts that bring you tears of joy, and those memories that make your heart glow.

Reclaim and take advantage of the power of your inner child by finding activities that your inner child loves and get involved in them. Whatever it is that you truly enjoy and that brings the best out of you, explore it. Reach for everything that sets your soul on fire: create, invent, explore, and innovate. Try things that scare you, step out of your comfort zone, and you may just be surprised by the dormant potential you discover. Allow yourself uncomplicated moments of creativity and play, and liberate yourself from the ties of expectations.

Life is not as complicated as we make it out to be. The best you can do is learn from the authentic and spontaneous child you once were. Reconnect with your inner self, your inner child, and tap back into happiness, joy, and peace.

5

EMBRACING PATIENCE & UNCERTAINTY

> "When you become comfortable with uncertainty, infinite possibilities open up in your life."
>
> — Eckhart Tolle

Experiments carried out about six decades ago revealed that when people have foreknowledge that they will be exposed to painful or discomforting situations, for example, an electric shock or an unpleasant image, they react far less than when they are exposed to these same conditions when they are not expecting it. This is due to the fact that uncertainty makes preparing for or controlling events difficult.

David Rock unveils some of the mechanisms of thought patterns in *Your Brain at Work,* in which he states that "the brain craves certainty. A sense of uncertainty about the future and feeling out of control both generate strong limbic system responses." (Rock, 2009) The limbic system, being (in part) responsible for emotional responses, is a powerful component of our make-up. Simply put, uncertainty tends to trigger adverse reactions. Being able to predict and anticipate events and our lives' happenings provides us with a sense of security. We are programmed to seek predictability to protect ourselves. Having to sit with the unknown or lose a sense of direction generates fear, which can provoke stress and anxiety as our minds struggle to cope with uncertainty.

According to researchers Dugas & Buhr (2009), "intolerance of uncertainty involves the tendency to react negatively on an emotional, cognitive, and behavioral level to uncertain situations and events." We are so afraid of not knowing what tomorrow may bring that this fear disrupts our long-term welfare and interferes with our emotional freedom.

In the time of our ancestors who were majorly hunters and gatherers, some of the uncertainties they had to contend with were the threat of being killed by wild animals, attacks from rival tribal groups, harsh climatic conditions, and disease outbreak. Fortunately, we no longer face the same obstacles to our survival... but that doesn't exclude a renewed and updated set of existential uncertainties. So many aspects of our lives – important ones at that – are not within our control. We navigate unpredictable waters every day of our lives, unsure about the solidity of our relationships, the stability and growth of our finances, and the maintenance of our health; job security is not a given, nor is a stable political and economic climate. These elements are not easy to deal with, and if we cannot cope with being in a continuous state of uncertainty, it undoubtedly affects our mental health.

At the core of ourselves, we all are afraid of the future,

mainly because we do not know what lies ahead. We tend to assume that things will continue to be as they are. Only, none of us are immune to change or adversity. Whether it makes our lives take a turn for better or worse, the transitional state that is brought on by change tends to leave us in considerable discomfort.

Lacking confidence in our ability to cope with unexpected events or situations often leads to avoidance and suppressing emotions. The multiple repercussions of this include mind negativity bias, which is how our negative emotions take precedence over positive ones when confronted with a situation. This becomes a very harmful habit and is highly detrimental to our emotional and mental wellbeing.

Although we may believe we lack the necessary life skills to navigate uncertainty, we all possess the ability to choose how we respond. You hold the power to intercept your thoughts before they meet your emotions, and you possess the ability to prevent them from dissolving and spreading within your inner space. Whether you choose to believe your thoughts is entirely up to you. Remember that believing in your decisional power and stepping in and taking charge of your emotional responses is a substantial first step in the right direction.

Now, even though all humans are faced with the same problem of uncertainty, the way we react to it differs. Understand that these reactions are our coping mechanisms and our way of dealing with uncertainty. Those who resort to worrying are choosing to play it safe with risks and potential threats. Furthermore, in situations of uncertainty, one of the common ways in which we cope is to do something that we feel gives us an illusion of being in control, such as excessive planning, obsessive cleaning, dictating what others must do, and basically micro-managing every area of your life.

Now, developing resilience is a huge factor in learning to sit with uncertainty. Having complete faith in yourself and knowing that you possess the capacity to bounce back from adversity is full-proof. With this conviction, nothing can truly stand in your way. Whatever happens, you know yourself enough to trust in your resourcefulness.

Also, building up your tolerance to change by taking risks and embrace discomfort can lead to a healthy way of coping. Hurdles will undoubtedly appear, but the more experience you have in facing them, the stronger you will be in meeting the challenges.

One sure thing about this world is its unavoidable and perilous uncertainty. No one knows what tomorrow holds. We cannot predict or control what others will do nor how others react. The best we can do is to take steps to confront the fear of uncertainty.

How to face **uncertainty**

Now, even though we know that allowing ourselves to feel our emotions - including uncertainty-related stress - can help us navigate stormy weather, there are other things we can do to maintain our calm and focus during these periods. Here a few simple tips to hold on to. Keep these in mind in times when you feel overwhelmed with uncontrollable events or when having to deal with unknown circumstances.

Exercise

Physical activities are an excellent outlet in so many

circumstances. Whether you feel wound-up or completely lethargic, intensive exercise can help stabilize your mood and clear your mind. Among many of its benefits, exercise increases blood flow, reduces cortisol (stress hormone) levels, increases the production of endorphins, and creates a sense of lightness and wellbeing. An intensive exercise session can help you tap back into your breathing and regulate your emotions. If you enjoy team sports all the best, this will provide a chance to connect with others and enjoy camaraderie while getting all the benefits of a workout.

Not feeling particularly athletic or in the mood for strenuous exertion? No worries. At whichever pace you choose, a long walk can be very soothing and can also be a moment to ground yourself through mindfulness.

Speak up

Surrounding ourselves with people who have a positive mindset is an excellent way to tap into it ourselves. Your tribe is everything. Think about one or more people you can turn to in times of need. These people cannot be those around you who are constantly inundated in drama or persistently negative. You might select family members, close friends, colleagues, or someone else you feel comfortable being yourself around, someone in which you can happily and easily confide.

Meditate

Taking a moment to pause and observe your thoughts can only be beneficial beyond expectations. Allocate some time every day to tap out of the hustle and bustle, and sit with yourself in a quiet spot. Introspection and thought observation are highly beneficial in gaining perspective. This will help view uncertainty from a different point of view, perhaps offering a soothing reassurance that all will come to pass, no matter how much of a struggle you put up. Furthermore, it provides a special moment to practice gratitude. Mediation is a wonderful opportunity to look back on your day and bring to light everything that you are grateful for, from the roof over your head to the caring people in your life.

Diversions

Unless used for avoidance, a diversion can be calming and help steer the focus away from the constant stress of uncertainty. Diversions include anything that entertains you, usually a hobby or pastime. Don't have a hobby? Find one! Reading, painting, gardening, watching movies, playing a musical instrument, dancing...the options are endless. Having something pleasant to turn to in times of stress can be life-changing.

Sort yourself out

Although an excessive amount of this can impede you from moving forward, a balanced approach can be relaxing and offer a sense of control. I am talking about tidying. Yes, cleaning, sorting and organizing; clearing, scrubbing, and washing. Although some people will retch at the idea of doing this for fun, it can procure a short-term sense of accomplishment and control over one's environment. Cleaning can be therapeutic, although it is handy to be aware that it can turn into an obsession. If this is your chosen coping method, perhaps you should add a hint of moderation to that cleaning solution.

. . .

Stop swimming against the current

Living with uncertainty can elicit existential crises in the manner of hopelessness, despair, and depression because of the feeling that your contributions amount to nothing. Many people struggle with this, a sense of powerlessness based on the future's unpredictable challenges. This is why we seek to control and avoid confrontation.

There are countless things that we cannot control or change, but one thing we can do is choose how we respond. You can decide to be your own most dependable and reliable person. You can choose to show up for yourself every single time.

Accepting the reality of uncertainty and being able to better manage it requires a change in perspective. The place to begin is to understand that yielding to the forces of life rather than opposing them can be a tremendous relief. Once you fully acknowledge that uncertainty is beyond your control, you can let yourself flow and experience life fully. It will most likely be uncomfortable at first, but surrendering to the natural order of things is a far easier and more beneficial option than fighting against them.

Sometimes we try to control our uncertainties through worrying and feeling anxious, fearful, or impatient. We may start overthinking things, which is highly inadvisable. Although it may seem like we are preparing for all possible outcomes within the circumstances, overthinking merely deepens the gap between being calm and collected, and ultimately losing control over our thoughts and emotional reactions. It confuses us and leads us to become embroiled in our fears and anxieties instead of logically reacting to them. A sufficient amount of stress can also activate our fight or flight response, through which our nervous system may mislead us into falsely interpreting a situation. What was initially a position of discomfort has now escalated into a full-blown emotional meltdown.

When we view a situation from a negative viewpoint and conclude that it will defeat us, we then operate from a position of fear. This is a sneaky way in which our body responds as it short circuits our brain, making us unable to regulate emotions and direct our focus. You can practice being open and accepting of challenges by reprogramming your thoughts. Using positive statements is an effective technique. Positive affirmations tend to lead to positive outcomes, or at least, they will look more positive from your viewpoint. Remember, most of what happens to us is reliant on perceptions. One same situation can be viewed differently by several people. Therefore, if you can't change the situation, why not alter your perception?

THE TRUTH IS, by fighting your reality and attempting to change things beyond your control, you are only making things worse. Now, giving up fighting does not mean giving up trying to make your life better in ways that you see fit! It simply means you need to reconnect with yourself and learn how to greet challenges differently. There is no need to complain; things are what they are. Life will always present a number of things that are out of your control, and that is absolutely fine because you can learn to cope healthily with anything that comes your way.

JUST FLOW

Adopting a flexible standpoint instead of being rigid has

been proven, time and again, to be the best and healthiest response to challenges. We need to come to terms with the fact that life itself isn't perfect and find peace with anything that is put in our path. We can study situations and learn our own lessons from them. Make peace with the fact that no matter your level of certainty about something, nothing is set in stone. If your initial reaction is disappointment, it is up to you to decide if you wish to live with this feeling or let it go. Let's work towards being content with not knowing everything. True happiness comes from our capacity to embrace the unknown, to enjoy and respect it, and learn to flow.

> "Uncertainty is the only certainty there is, and knowing how to live with insecurity is the only security."
>
> — John Allen Paulos

There is a mental state concept called *flow,* which was coined by Hungarian-American author and psychologist Mihaly Csikszentmihalyi. In his search to determine what makes a life worth living following traumatic events and the loss of everything you hold dearly, Csikszentmihalyi began to investigate different patterns that might determine happiness. In doing so, he discovered that many people felt an incomparable sense of fulfillment when they were in this altered state of mind, a state that made them feel at one with what they were doing. The psychologist recalls interviewing a music composer who would get lost in a state of complete oneness with his music when composing. Flow is a situation where time ceases to exist, described by Csikszentmihalyi as "the state of total immersion while doing an activity." In his recent work, he also indicates that "flow comes from the intense concentration around your own actions and their immediate feedback." (Csikszentmihalyi, 2008)

KEEPING THIS IN MIND, perhaps we can try to recall when in our lives we have been in that state. Flow usually occurs when we are doing something engaging, something we are passionate about, and of which we are fluent and knowledgeable. When, in everyday life, do we actually feel happy, excited, inspired? Csikszentmihalyi revealed that many reaped the benefits of happiness not by doing things that brought them fame or fortune, but by being engaged in something they loved, during which they felt like the world has stopped.

It has been suggested that real happiness and contentment come from being so involved in a process that we lose sight of other things; it is a mental state of complete and energized focus. We are so immersed in what we are doing that we become unaware of other distracting factors.

We spend so much time worrying about things that have barely anything to do with us, as well as situations that we have no control over. What we must do is follow the advice of Steve Marabol, who advises: "You must learn to let go. Release the stress. You were never in control anyway." He is telling us to stop trying to keep a firm hold on people, things, and events. It is a losing battle, one that will exhaust and stress you beyond measure. In time, this takes a horrible toll on our minds and bodies.

. . .

THIS LEADS us to our next point: when our reactions to uncertainty are not adaptive, we cannot expect to flow with the current. Opting for an adaptive approach allows us to just go with it; to adjust how we respond in a smooth, centered, and balanced manner. This does not imply being entirely passive, but simply to let go of what you cannot control. Flow teaches us that whatever happens, no matter our lives' circumstances, we can always tap into this inner power. Flow is pure passion, pure being, absolute presence in the moment.

Be ready to engage with your issues. Sit with your uncertainty and let it pass through.

Imagine yourself floating like a starfish in pristine turquoise waters. As your body moves to the rhythm of the swell, you float upwards and down, unknowing of what the next wave will bring. Perhaps it will submerge you and take you under, only for a moment, or maybe longer. Maybe it will raise you higher and higher, anticipation and excitement filling your soul.

Such is the way of life; a series of motions, riding the waves of the unknown, hoping for the best while accepting the extent of possibilities. Everything comes to pass, so it is up to you to choose how you want to go through the storm. You could choose to focus on the possible negative outcomes of any situation or decide to try your best with what you actually know, using the tools at hand. You could focus on what might be and what might have been, but wouldn't it be more productive to concentrate your energy on what is here in the now? Through involvement and engagement, we learn the lessons that life has in store for us; no growth can come from avoidance. Be at peace with the unknown; welcome it, respect it, and enjoy it. Let things flow. Create a unique experience for yourself and live your life to the fullest.

. . .

The Power of Resilience

No matter its evolution level, the human brain is designed to protect you, and it does this by underestimating the positive while overestimating the negative. We are often drawn to negativity because it provokes a reaction within us. Negative news such as job loss, death, and economic collapse puts our brains on high alert and allows us to prepare for negative outcomes.

Although this is how we naturally view and respond to life's challenges, fighting and avoiding are not advisable ways to approach adversity.

Resilience is the ability to bounce back. It is your ability to get back up after a fall and rise stronger as you move towards your future. Only by facing adversity and surrounding ourselves with love can we build resilience. Furthermore, I will repeat this; it is crucial to face our traumas and deal with emotions if we want to move forward, into a comfortable place within ourselves. In fact, resilience expert Boris Cyrulnik mentions, "Triggering a process of resilience is about escaping the prison of our past." (Cyrulnik, 2020) Greeting each day as a clean slate, without dwelling on past mistakes or misfortunes, is an essential factor for healing and mental wellbeing.

Our beliefs affect what we see and the way we interpret situations. Outcomes are not always within our control. We can battle through life to keep controlling everything that happens to us, or we can experience life fully, floating through, making decisions to the best of our knowledge, and have our own backs when things go sour. Extend the favors and appreciation you would offer a good friend to yourself. Why not? Why not be our own hero, our own best friend? There is no shame in feeling whole. As a matter of fact, it makes it easier to admit our mistakes, forgive our past, and move forward. It makes it easier to build resilience. It makes for more authentic relationships and a complete sense of self.

This is the basis of resilience. It is the capacity to respond to the challenges of life by being flexible and adaptive. Go ahead, let yourself float mindfully through the motions. Accept things as they are, through a state of equanimity.

Our set of unconscious and conscious beliefs create this type of mindset. This can determine how you respond in moments of uncertainty, how you perceive yourself, and how you relate to others. This mindset is a totality of who you are and how you tell your story.

YOU WILL BE able to perceive things more clearly because of your ability to float mindfully through the motions of life, in such a manner that you are not focused on what is going on around you but rather on that which is going on inside you. It leaves room for perspective and allows for a unique connection into yourself, as it is a way to see further than what your eyes are telling you.

So many important lessons can be taken away from unfortunate circumstances. If you can see past your misfortunes, you may find an abundance of lessons in disguise. Seek opportunities to learn about yourself, about your strengths and weaknesses, and how you react to distressing situations. Being able to embrace your challenges mindfully and learn from them will pave the way for wisdom.

Such is the way of life; a series of motions, riding the waves of the unknown, hoping for the best while accepting the extent of possibilities. Uncertainty is unavoidable. To make the most of our short time here, we must turn to acceptance rather than resistance. Adjusting to the motions and being adaptive is crucial to gaining perspective. Everything comes to pass, so it is up to you to choose how you want to go through the storm.

6

GROWING PAINS

> "Out of your vulnerabilities will come your strength."
>
> — Sigmund Freud

One of the characteristics of a living being is growth. Whether it is physical, emotional, mental, or social, this characteristic is ever-present. As we all scramble to figure out our lives and provide a sense to our existence, we undoubtedly experience ups and downs. Some of us rise very high and crash very low. Others keep a steady, uneventful pace – which is not necessarily a bad thing. As you move forward and create your path, you are building yourself – up or down – as you remove some bits and adjust others. Sometimes we see ourselves having to remove big chunks of "us," such as relationships that may no longer serve us. Sometimes we replace pieces, take out the old unproductive or pointless parts, upgrade to a new way of being, or perhaps adopt a new perspective. Now, we all want to be able to move from where we are to another point as fast as we can. Wouldn't it be nice to get there sooner, to skip through the discomfort and pain of break-ups, dieting, adopting a new exercise regimen, and confronting family members? The truth is that it cannot be done by the snap of a finger. Shortcuts rarely provide the same outcome and benefits as taking the long road. Doing the work builds strength. You cannot gain strength without building resistance. That's not how things work, physically and mentally. We must go through the process of traveling the distance between these two points. We must attempt to make it past the ups and downs in order to come out stronger, through failures and successes.

So, how can we go about this inward growth process? In the first place, it is about adopting an open-minded attitude. This allows for new ideas to be noticed and considered. It leaves space for the 'new' to come in, and as it tries to make its way into your life, you will notice the old patterns, relationships, and thoughts that are no longer of service. These will be discarded to create new space, and you will be able to greet opportunities openly. Remaining open-minded and keeping a positive focus on things that matter can alter your entire approach to life. It will shift you from a 'can't do' perspective to a 'can do' mindset.

Getting rid of unproductive and limiting thought patterns, such as chronic negativity or constant apprehension, will ultimately steer you towards opportunities and positivity.

Strive to become yourself and conquer any obstacle that will prevent that from happening. Let go of what you can't control, stop complaining, and dwelling on your past. Dismiss procrastination – it is the ultimate trap! Face life head-on; each day is for you to seize.

Now, growing out of our old ways and shedding our spurious identities is not an easy feat. This growth process is not only challenging but also painful. Shedding off these limiting parts of us may imply facing certain truths that we have been avoiding. It may mean sacrificing relationships that no longer serve us, and it may lead us to question everything we've held for certain since our youth. There's a pain that greets the action of peeling off a part of us that we have known for years to reveal who we are underneath the lies, self-doubts, and untruths. It is comparable to trying to break free from the hold of addiction.

But only through shedding its skin can a caterpillar eventually become a butterfly.

Obstacles to living **your truth**

Humans are anatomically, biochemically, and physiologically the same, but even with this similarity in morphology, we are all very different individuals.

So many factors influence who we are and who we eventually become. Everyone has a unique life path. Our differences are what make us exactly who we are; they characterize our individuality. Yet, we are much too often willing to dismiss our authenticity to gain external approval and please others. Indeed there's another way to feel accepted and live our truth.

The fact is, we can only feel like our own true selves when we fully express these differences and live in full truthfulness and openness. Living your truth implies fully embracing yourself as a person. No matter what you do, there will always be judgment. Can you shine your uniqueness past the comments and criticism of your peers?

Remember to beware of perfectionism. It is a trap and is merely the result of incessant self-doubt. You are not here to reach for and fulfill the potential of others. Live by your rules, by that which you believe in and put into practice. Abide by your personal values, the ones you've established, the ones that you nurture and set forth in every aspect of your life. It is crucial that you live your truth as it is the foundation upon which you build your life. It will influence everything - your relationships, your career, your emotions, and your wellbeing. Not living by your convictions can be likened to building a life based on a foundation of untruths, fabrications, misinterpretations, and denial.

As good as living your truth can be, many obstacles may stand in your way. All these stumbling blocks can prevent you from being your real self if you allow them to do so. A few of the obstacles that impede our ability to speak our minds may be linked to judgment, societal conventions, social pressure, family values and expectations, and mental health stigmas. However, when it comes to your boundaries, you always have the final verdict. Complying with others' demands and wishes is not the only option for living peacefully and feeling accepted. There are ways to experiment and grow into this. Opting for self-affirmation rather than people-pleasing is daunting at first and tends to stir up insecurities, which can make us feel worse than we initially felt. But if approached in a scaled, mindful manner, self-affirmation can lead to more respectful relationships and a well-rounded sense of belonging.

Every opinion and judgment that is not serving you,

whether they are external or internal judgment, must be removed. Judgment has the capacity to let you doubt yourself and so prevent your true potential from bursting out.

Speak your mind! You are unique, and so you should express your truth. Not only is this an essential aspect of your personal development, but it is also incredibly valuable to others. The more you stand your ground and speak your mind, the more others around you will feel comfortable following in your steps. Within respectful parameters, expressing different opinions and ideas can lead to more openness, acceptance, non-judgment, the betterment of self, and innovation.

It would be a fallacy to claim that we are all born the same; on some level, we are, but it is clear that socioeconomic status is a strong indicator of which road we will follow in life. Unfortunately, social conventions, capitalism, and the media's influence are powerful components of our world. All of these affect our emotional wellbeing and act as guidelines to our belief systems. This makes us believe we should act, look, and live a certain way.

On the other hand, you don't have to claim authority, be very wealthy, or have political or social influence to be your true self. An over-inflated ego and the ability to use it to one's advantage does not exonerate someone from possessing all primary human attributes. On some foundational level, we are all equal. Your value is yours to create.

The idea is not for you to design a new system of living your life. It is intended to rid yourself of the need to fit into a mold designed to keep us within a particular frame. If following the crowd implies sacrificing your ethics and morals, perhaps it is not as beneficial to your wellbeing as you may have believed. In time, you can learn to distinguish that which will be in your best interest and discard all that isn't beneficial.

The power of NO

There are deeply ingrained patterns of needing to please others that are sabotaging our sense of self. When we grow up with this "need to please" mindset, it is difficult to break out of the pattern. The belief that what makes us good enough to be loved or respected by others is their ability to comply with their demands and wishes. We can easily get lost between what is true, what is right, and the authentic expression of our thoughts. Contenting others should not come at a personal cost.

Continuously relying on external validation has its price to pay; it is the ultimate sacrifice of your true self. Think about it: unable to internally validate yourself, you turn to others to order or confirm your thoughts, words, and actions. Where are *you* underneath all of this? There can be no sense of self-value or self-respect without a full understanding of self, governed by internal validation. Only you can know your truth, only you can own it, and only you can speak it. No one else has walked in your shoes, nor will they ever. In case you are still in doubt, this is a gentle reminder that people speak in accordance with their own baggage, issues, and self-concept. You can never offend someone unless they *choose* to take offense. Outside perspectives usually have nothing to do with you, as people tend to think of others as representations of themselves. Some advice and outside perspectives might be helpful, but ultimately it is up to you to decide what meets your needs and how to get there.

. . .

THE CHILDHOOD SCRIPT of living your life just to gratify others' needs to be discarded and rewritten. You can no longer afford to live your life like this. Learning to say NO, loud and clear, is a beautiful gift you must offer yourself. Refusing to make choices based on what people want and expect of you will change your life. Will it be challenging? Sure. Actually, it will most definitely be testing at first. But just like any habit, as you develop your strength of character and self-assuredness, you will witness how people adapt to the standards you've set. And what about those who can't stand the heat? They usually end up leaving the kitchen. Just think of how empowering and rewarding it will be to claim yourself back. Like every step in this growth process, it will take courage, determination, and resilience. Throughout this process, you will find peace of mind and a sense of wellbeing as you claim control over your life, your choices, and their outcomes.

When we ceaselessly attempt to please others, we deprive ourselves of keeping hold of valuable pieces of our authentic being. Being overly agreeable can come at a dear price. It is often a sacrifice of self-respect, integrity, self-esteem, and identity. It generates negative feelings towards oneself, constantly criticizing and belittling what we think and do. Shame, one of the most damaging emotional states, is also a derivation of being unable to set boundaries. Brené Brown says it best: "I define shame as the intensely painful feeling or experience of believing that we are flawed and therefore unworthy of love and belonging – something we've experienced, done, or failed to do makes us unworthy of connection." (Brown, 2013) Persistently viewing yourself as lesser than others and not good enough is harmful to the mind and the body. What's more, chronic insecurity leaves you at the mercy of others' better judgment – which is not a safe and happy place to be.

THIS HAS BEEN one of the biggest battles of my life, and I am no longer ashamed to say that it is an ongoing recovery process. We are not programmed to stand tall to be strong and to take pride. Somehow along the way, humility has become a synonym for belittling ourselves so as not to offend others' pride. I now understand and remind myself constantly that the contentment of others cannot be detrimental to my wellbeing. Why should I respect others and not my own person? In that aspect, we must put ourselves first. I encourage you to use the tools offered here (reflection, mediation, talk therapy) to find comfort in self-validation. Understand that you are enough; that you are worthy of love, respect, and dignity, just as is anyone else.

Learning to say NO is pure art. The workings around self-affirmation are complex. For some of us, it comes easily; for others, it is the battle of a lifetime. In situations of doubt as to whether you are being true to yourself or merely being agreeable, you can opt to remove yourself and think about what you want and what feels right. And if this creates an adverse reaction from the other party involved, I would like to remind you that it does not matter. Others are entitled to express their emotions, and this is never a reflection on you. I like to think that we don't owe anything but respect. Refusing to make life choices based on what people want from you is the most important, reflecting respect for oneself.

RECOGNIZING **toxicity**

The term "toxic" is often used to describe substances capable of causing severe harm and debilitation. In our quest to reconnect with our true selves, we must learn to recognize toxicity in our environment. Toxicity can be found in many forms, including destructive relationships, an unhealthy work environment, and self-damaging habits. It can often be attributed to negative places, behaviors, thoughts, and individuals.

Once you've established your fundamental principles and boundaries, these toxic patterns in your life tend to become more evident. This is not surprising, as, at this point, you will feel more in control of your needs and wants, making it possible to see clearly that which does not serve you.

When these unwanted aspects of your life begin to appear, you will be confronted with difficult choices. It can be challenging and daunting to accept that some habits and people are no longer beneficial to your wellbeing. It may feel like a revelation, but deep down, we all know that our intuitive self was light years ahead of our consciousness. At this stage, you will undoubtedly need to take some time to pause and reflect. You may find it useful to whip out a piece of paper and jot down the positive versus negative for every element you doubt. In doing this, remember that not all confronting aspects need to be immediately discarded. It is up to you to reach inwards into your intuitive self, as well as into your rational self, to determine what will bring you emotional balance.

Some indicators can help us pinpoint what is not of service to us. Feeling worse after an interaction can sometimes be an indicator of toxicity. Whatever it is that manipulates you, takes advantage of you for their own benefit, makes you feel less of yourself, and causes abuse or harm to you in any way can be said to bring toxicity into your life.

. . .

As a general guideline, elements that bring out the worst in you should be eliminated from your life. For example, if one of your personal values is to act and speak positively whenever possible, you may want to stay away from people who cultivate and thrive on negativity. There is much truth in the proverb "misery likes company." We attract what we encompass and project to the world. Furthermore, it is part of human nature to seek that which is familiar or alike. Knowing this, the power is in your hands to create an environment you can thrive in and to reach your full potential in accordance with your values.

Now, understand that being toxic may sometimes not mean that people or environments are fundamentally wrong, but simply that they are harmful to you. Those unhealthy patterns may only appear when you interact with them... and that's ok! We are all different and have distinct needs. These elements don't have to be labeled as "bad," but instead dismissed as not being of service to you. With this neutral mindset, it becomes easy to release toxicity without feeling guilt, sadness, or frustration.

Shifting your perceptions

The mind can be likened to a stream. Just like the water that flows through, your thoughts waver in and out. Just as a stream flows without anyone's input or control, thoughts also tend to drift in and out of your mind without being pushed to do so. They come from everywhere and nowhere. They can leave a deep imprint or vanish like dust.

Every second of each day, this stream flows steadily.

You don't create your thoughts, but you do experience

them. In that sense, you have no power to select most of what may pop into your mind, but you do possess the ability to choose how you react to your thoughts. There are many strategies linked to the practice of mindfulness and meditation that facilitate the regulation of emotional responses. Being aware of our thoughts and consciously holding on to or dismissing them takes practice.

When you are operating from a position of unawareness, you can't observe your thoughts and realize which ones to hold on to. You are only reacting to things that pop into your head. As a result, you become swept away by them, as well as by the emotional response they resuscitate.

Identifying your thoughts is an essential first step in regulating your response. When you pay attention to a specific idea, perhaps one that is bothering you, you are already acknowledging its existence. This then enables you to make a conscious decision as to whether you will allow it to permeate your emotions or let it float on and back to where it came from. If you were to speak to that thought, it would sound something like this: "I know you are there, but you are not real. You are not needed. Please move along and away." The same goes for thoughts that serve your purpose; you might decide to hold on to those that will benefit you. The point is, you are not a victim of your thoughts, but rather the ultimate decider. Cultivating such a frame of mind will help you develop awareness and shift perceptions, making it possible to push aside judgment and preconceived ideas.

THE COMPARISON TRAP

> "Comparison is the thief of joy."

— Theodore Roosevelt

OUR DIFFERENCES ARE what make us strong and allow us to distinguish ourselves from the crowd. Comparing ourselves to others in order to measure how well we are moving along through life is a habit we develop from an early age. We've all been condition to follow certain societal parameters, this intangible guideline labeled normality. What, in fact, does it mean to be "normal"? What is usually attributed to the spectrum of normality refers to that which is average, that of which most people adhere to. Normality is highly subjective and varies in different societal frames. Normality also implies conformity, and as we've previously explored, conformity is one way in which we lose our sense of self.

When you compare yourself to other people, whether based on job performance, wealth, looks, social abilities, or even social media popularity, you are disempowering yourself. It is impossible to stand your ground and live authentically while you are comparing yourself to others. To live a full life in a complete self-expanded state, the only fruitful comparison you should make is to your old self.

Focusing on others' achievements or successes can be beneficial if it inspires us to move forward. However, comparisons tend to reflect that which we yearn for, or wish to be, which leads to victimizing ourselves. We unknowingly place ourselves in a "lesser" category, creating those limiting thought patterns. This is a fast track to chronic dissatisfaction and unhappiness. All it ever does is keep us focused on what we hate about ourselves and our lives. It steals away valuable energy, time, and effort that would have been better expended on building a better tomorrow. If only that energy could be shifted into observing our own potential and working towards bettering ourselves in accordance with our goals and principles, we could become unstoppable. It is surprising how often the most significant obstacles to living a fulfilling life are within our self.

You have to take back your power, which you have given away to people, situations, and places. To move past this incessant comparing, you must make a clear and conscious choice to clean up your self-deprecating thoughts. Because that is, in fact, precisely what you are submitting yourself to when you belittle yourself in such a way. Others are free to succeed or fail; the way they live their lives has no connection to your potential to change yours. Decide not to waste your time and energy on others, but rather use it to build yourself up. Drive your focus towards being the best possible version of yourself.

When in doubt, recall all the obstacles you have already overcome. Remember your victories and celebrate how much you have progressed on your personal voyage. Life is a journey, not a race. Enjoy each step, as there are valuable teachings at every stage. Start every new day with a clean slate. You have the power to alter the future, beginning with a fresh start every minute, every single day. Whenever you are confronted with a dilemma, see it as a gift. Making choices is creating opportunities.

This is a valuable habit to put into practice. Comparing yourself to others should no longer serve you. Find that space within yourself where you can cultivate appreciation, kindness, and gratitude for what you have accomplished.

Collateral Damage

No other aptitude is worthier than that of truly knowing yourself. Being your authentic self means owning your own reality. It implies unapologetically acknowledging, accepting, and loving your imperfections. It is choosing to speak and live your truth and being whole and happy about it instead of living for the acceptance and gratification of others. As a natural consequence of growing into your true self, your energy will shift, and you will realize that some people and things no longer serve your purpose and so should no longer be a part of your life.

Until you are your real and authentic self, you cannot live your best life. Confidence and total fulfillment come from truly knowing yourself. Make decisions that improve and better your life, rather than endlessly tending to the desires of others. Find what you want, and cultivate the courage to go and get it.

One thing you must know is that the road to becoming this person isn't paved with gold. Knowing where you stand and refusing to cross boundaries is not an easy route to follow. Arriving at the point where you are nothing but your true self will demand some sacrifices and challenge your character's strength in many ways. Be prepared to have to step out of your comfort zone. It will be a crucial step in becoming the person you really are, deep down. And don't think that this will always be a challenge; as the saying goes, *practice makes perfect*. As you put into place that which you choose to adhere to and act in full support of your values and principles, you will notice an evolution take place. You will see that some things that previously felt daunting have become a natural habit.

On your journey, there will be many things of which to let go and many other new ones to embrace. Mistakes will be made, have no doubt! But you will develop the strength to greet these mistakes with compassion and view them as learning opportunities.

On a final note, remember that you always have the choice to hold on to something or to let go. As you grow into your new soul skin, you will begin to perceive things differently, causing you to be driven to shed what does not serve the real YOU.

Although the freedom to be your true self is fulfilling, the work one must do to achieve that state of liberty can feel terrifying. Hold on to your conviction that the challenges it brings are absolutely and completely worth it. Keep your goals and aspirations at the forefront of your mind. And please, remember that you are worth it.

7

BODY & MIND

> "To keep the body in good health is a duty... otherwise we shall not be able to keep our mind strong and clear."
>
> — BUDDHA

THE RELATIONSHIP between the mind and the body is not a recent discovery. Until the 17th century, the mind and the body were treated as one unique and indivisible whole. Although the Western world's ideas about the lack of connection between the body and the mind led to significant medical advances, it experienced stunted growth in areas of emotional, psychological, and spiritual development. The healing of the physical body was connected to extrinsic factors, such as surgery and medication. This attitude towards medicine and treatment continued until the

20th century. As things began to change, research work surfaced in the area of connections between the mind and the body. The research showed a complex but essential link between these two parts of our making. Out of this emerged a new discourse, proclaiming the benefits of mind-body practices.

I cannot tell you how many times I have been a victim of a mind-body-associated breakdown. As a child, I would spend countless hours at day-care lying on the floor in a quiet corner, attempting to cope with an endless stream of headaches and migraines. I was taken to numerous doctors, had scans and tests performed; yet, no physical ailment was ever found to be a trigger. As a teenager, I struggled with much anxiety, and these cyclical migraines persisted in making an appearance. Headaches were a daily occurrence.

Years passed, and I struggled with stress and anxiety, headaches becoming a central part of my daily life. Towards my later teen years, I joined an organized sports team, which led to me being much more active. This also created a sense of belonging within a new group of friends. High doses of strenuous physical activity combined with positive social interaction turned out to be most helpful in attenuating my headaches' frequency and strength. Much of my angst had come from not having a sense of purpose and belonging, which was appeased by this passion I had discovered.

Now, I only came to this realization many years later as an adult. I was going through a period of several life-changes that had me feeling powerless, confused as to where I belonged, and anxious. This left me in a very vulnerable state, and migraines had me feeling helpless; I could not control them, and I did not know how to prevent them. Deciding I could not live my life this way, I began to change my diet and returned to daily high-intensity exercise. I set about making plans to continue traveling abroad, which had always been one of my heart's deepest desires.

When I finally set out to do things my way, follow my dreams, and lead with my heart, I unleashed a dormant potential. I realized that when my mind was strong and fulfilled, my body responded in much the same way. My headaches still appeared at times, but I recognized them as a friend tapping me on the shoulder, saying, "maybe you should reconsider what you're doing." And the truth is, sometimes I didn't listen and pushed forward anyway, avoiding my intuition and following my rational thoughts. And every single time, a migraine ensued.

If there is any advice I can offer from what I have learned, it is that our minds and bodies are connected in such a privileged way that it would be shameful to dismiss the signals we receive. Our physical body and psyche are interlinked and are continuously communicating messages to us, responding to our environment in view of where we stand. Although my life's challenges have revolved around releasing anxiety patterns, everyone has their own particular battles to fight. Remember that it is a battle in which your greatest ally lies within you; you may as well acknowledge its presence and make the most of it.

The link between physical and psychological wellbeing

The complex interrelationship between the body and the mind means that your feelings, thoughts, attitudes, and beliefs have a direct relationship with the way your body works. In fact, we could almost say that our bodies respond to our psyche. Your mind impacts your body, whether negatively or positively.

Understanding this link does not permit us to heal all our

physical wounds instantly. It does, however, provide us with an opportunity to investigate the benefits of holistic healing. It can help us gain insight into our general health and offer us an alternative to modern medicinal practices. Many mind-body practices have no negative repercussions whatsoever and can help cultivate a balanced lifestyle. Body-mind practices such as meditation, mindfulness, massage therapy, and yoga can be founded on the interrelationship between these two parts of the body. The mind affects the body, and the body affects the mind. Knowledge of alternative and preventive healing methods is empowering. Understanding the intricate workings of our body and mind allows us to make better informed health-oriented decisions. This also shifts the responsibility of our holistic wellbeing from medical practitioners back into our own hands.

Optimal wellbeing promotes the synchronistic work between the physical (body) and the psychological (mind). There exists a complex relationship between physical and mental wellbeing, as the physical part of the body is interconnected to the psychological part.

The World Health Organization's constitution happens to indicate that "Health is a state of complete physical, mental and social wellbeing and not merely the absence of disease or infirmity. There is no health without mental health." (WHO, 1946) In that sense, veritable wellbeing consists of seamless interconnectivity between these aspects, a state of dynamic balance to create complete harmony within our being – which is all the more reason to implement holistic approaches when it comes to promoting our health and preventing diseases.

In trying to understand this mind-body connection, let's start by making some clarifications. The first thing is this: the mind isn't the same thing as the brain. Although they are intricately connected, the mind consists of mental states such as thoughts, emotions, beliefs, memories, attitudes, and desires. The mind is nonphysical, whereas the brain itself acts more like the hardware that makes it possible for these mental states to be experienced. Since these experiences are located in the body (not just in the brain), we can say the mind is in the body.

The hormones coursing through the body shape provoke and result from thoughts and emotions. For instance, testosterone brings out our competitive and self-focused side, yet it is also released when needed to reach these same outcomes. Adrenaline can make us energized or anxious, as well as being one of our stress-response protection mechanisms. Endorphins can be released with intense exercise, offering an overwhelming sense of lightness and wellbeing. Interestingly, we also possess neurotransmitters in our gut that help us respond and remember experiences, providing the physiological foundation of gut feelings and intuition.

Our immune system is, in some way, an extension of the mind by how it influences our mood and responds to psychological stress. The mind and body are connected in a constant flow of inputs and outputs. At once, they experience the cause and the consequence of our thoughts and bodily responses. What this tells us is that a healthy and happy life results from a balanced relationship between physical and psychological states. One example of this is how people who exercise regularly sleep better, are more alert and enjoy a greater sense of wellbeing. The body and mind are interconnected, and both perform significant roles in determining how we think, how we act, and the way in which we experience life.

. . .

Gut-brain connection

Our digestive system, commonly referred to as our gut, is a central part of our physical composition. Your digestive system is responsible for vital bodily responses. Having a major influence on the development and reactions of our immune system, our gut has many functions. It is most commonly known for facilitating digestion and absorbing nutrients but does so much more. Lined with over 100 trillion bacteria and 100 million neurons, your gut is home to over 70% of your body's immunity cells. It produces a substantial number of neurotransmitters that directly connect your gut to your mind. Furthermore, over 95% of your body's serotonin, a chemical that regulates mood, is located in your gut. Often underestimated, your gut holds a predominant role in your overall mental and physical health.

What you feed your body and your mind will directly impact every aspect of your life. When your body is in good shape, you are more likely to feel in control, mentally strong, and alert. Whatever is detrimental to your mental health will often negatively impact your body and vice versa. An unwell mind can manifest its discomfort through the physical body: muscle pain, headaches, back pain, stomach ulcers, and neck stiffness – the list goes on. By understanding the link that exists between our physical and psychological wellbeing, we can opt for lifestyle choices that allow us to better manage our mental and physical health.

8

LIVING AUTHENTICALLY

> "The privilege of a lifetime is to become who you truly are."
>
> — Carl Jung

In a world driven by screen-obsession, networking, capitalism, status, ego, and materialism, talking about authenticity can feel like a foreign concept.

Many people have so buried themselves in following the crowd that they have no idea what being themselves actually means. We are majorly followers, forced to comply with certain measures to become a functioning member of modern society. In doing so, it has been easy to dismiss our exact needs and to set aside our inner-truth.

Living authentically is about approaching life from a different perspective; it is about living life from the inside out. A life of genuine authenticity is one where our feelings, thoughts, and actions are in harmony. It is living through a state of congruency, aligning our words and actions with our beliefs and principles.

Living authentically is about being ourselves, and that must come from a place of knowing ourselves. This implies identifying your true values and beliefs and then directing your actions and words to align with them. When you're living authentically, you enjoy an inner sense of peace, contentment, and meaning. If your words and actions are not aligned with your principles and beliefs, you will come to experience internal distress. When you are in this state of cognitive dissonance, your only options to deal with this sense of unpleasantness are to change your behavior or alter your thought patterns. Your peace can be restored when your external and internal worlds align. This self-knowledge requires self-awareness, self-acceptance, and mindfulness, all of which can be developed at any stage of life.

Personal values and beliefs are not what you should be or what you should do. They come from a place of knowing deep within and are a reflection of what you hold dear. Authenticity is having values that truly represent you at your best, the genuine person you want to be, and the most veritable version of yourself. It is having beliefs that reflect how you want to go about your life, rather than what you are told you should be. The truth is, authenticity leaves no space for external compliance.

> "Happiness depends upon ourselves."
>
> — Aristotle

DESIGN your happiness

One of Western society's most prevalent aspects is a culture of entitlement. This is a belief that external factors are somehow responsible for our happiness, as well as the outcomes of our life. There is a tendency to transfer responsibilities to greater entities, such as blaming laws, education, financial crises, and political decisions for our lack of self-fulfillment. It is relatively easy to push the blame onto external factors, thus justifying our lack of action to direct our own lives.

Many of us have been brought up to outsource responsibility for our lives, to reach out to others for self-validation and life-direction. Blame for our unhappiness has been laid upon our parents, teachers, bosses, spouses, friends, colleagues, and countless other factors. It is our responsibility to create and build the fortress of our existence.

THE TRUTH IS that you are and always will be the only person who can determine the quality of your life. Even though the outcomes are not always within our control, we possess the power to choose how we'll ride the waves of life. Your reactions are 100% your responsibility, dictating how you experience anything and everything that comes your way and whether it is a failure or a success. You are responsible for your achievements, losses, quality of relationships, health, physical fitness level, feelings, financial situation, and psychological well-being. I cannot stress this enough: your life is entirely your responsibility.

As a side note, while creating and designing a life for ourselves, we must be selective of the people we invite to accompany us on our journey. The people you spend most of your time with have a powerful impact in determining who you will become. Make a habit of mixing with people who will raise you instead of dragging you down. It is your responsibility to completely disentangle yourself from anyone whose values or beliefs are not aligned with your own. Surround yourself with friends, family, and colleagues who act as a healthy support system – people who accept you exactly as you are and have your best interest at heart.

In addition, remember that "you are the average of the five people you associate with most, so do not underestimate the effects of your pessimistic, unambitious, or disorganized friends. If someone isn't making you stronger, they're making you weaker." (Ferris, 2007) Reach out to those who will enhance your castle, and be fearless in turning away the people or things that do not serve your kingdom. Do things that speak to your soul; this will inevitably attract like-minded people and opportunities aligned with your objectives. The type of people you allow in will be extremely influential in determining whether you remain connected to your authentic self.

For far too long, we have blamed circumstances – favorable or unfavorable – as the reason for the many happenings in our lives. Living authentically is about understanding that you are your own choice. It's about knowing that there is a correlation between action and reaction, seed and fruit, sowing, and reaping. It is knowing that you are not a victim of your circumstances but are, in fact, a product of your decisions. As per the wise words of Epictetus, Greek philosopher: "Circumstances do not make the man, they only reveal him to himself."

. . .

Upsize your potential

Humans are created for expression; it has been in our nature since the beginning of time. The only way the world can enjoy the brilliance of your truest self is through its expression. In trying to avoid judgment or protecting others' feelings, many get into the self-defeating habit of downplaying their spark.

Downplaying your strengths for the benefit of others, whether this might lead to acceptance or success, is a losing game. Judgment from others is absolutely unavoidable. Everyone is their own unique person and is entitled to possess different perceptions and opinions. As such, in making yourself less than who you truly are, you are denying yourself full ownership of your person. You are standing in your own way on your path to living a self-accomplished fulfilling life.

Downplaying your potential will prevent you from fully expressing or experiencing anything that comes your way. The truth is that no matter what you do, you will never be able to please everyone. So, you might as well make decisions that reflect your innermost values and be your own best ally. Acknowledging your worth is not bragging, nor is it something of which to feel ashamed. Recognize yourself as your best ally, and use your many strengths to your advantage.

BECOMING YOU

The biggest and most significant discovery we can ever undertake is that of who we truly are. As important as this journey is, only a few of us contemplate it, and even less take on this challenge. Some may view this as an inherently selfish thing to do, failing to understand the beauty of this selfless act. However, as we begin to embrace our authentic selves, we become capable of offering the best of our being to those who matter most to us. This all begins at the source, at the very core of ourselves. To find fulfilment and purpose, we must start by discovering who we are. Striving to build your life on a solid foundation of self-love and self-knowledge is of great importance and a most noble feat.

On a final note, I would like to remind you that your journey to authenticity is unique, just as you are. In the words of Anna Quindlen, "the thing that is really hard, and really amazing, is giving up on being perfect and beginning to work on becoming yourself." Take that leap into yourself.

That is the true beauty of existence: being different, completely unique, perfectly flawed, and a beautiful work-in-progress. Acknowledging our wholeness and being kind and compassionate towards ourselves is a beautiful place to start.

POSTSCRIPT

Leave a Review

As an independent author with a small marketing budget, reviews are my livelihood on this platform. If you enjoyed this book, I would truly appreciate if you left your honest feedback. You can do this by clicking the link to the *Awakening to Authenticity Collection* on www.amazon.com .

Additionally, you can join our community here https://www.facebook.com/groups/theemeraldsociety, or contact me directly via ydgardens@emeraldsocpublishing.com.

I love hearing from my readers and I personally read every single review.

Stay well & strong.

Kindly,

YasD.

REFERENCES

Brown, B. (2017). *Braving the Wilderness: the quest for true belonging and the courage to stand alone*. Penguin Books.

Goleman, D. (1995). *Emotional Intelligence: Why it can matter more than IQ*. Bantam Books.

Brown, B. (2010). *The Gifts of Imperfection: Let go of who you think you're supposed to be and embrace who you are.* Hazelden Publishing.

Ferris, T. (2007). *The 4-Hour Work Week: Escape the 9-5, Live Anywhere and Join the New Rich*. Ebury Digital.

Brown, B. (2007). *I Thought It Was Just Me (but it isn't): Making the journey from "What Will People Think?" to "I Am Enough"*. Avery, Penguin Random House.

Kornfield, Jack. (2008). *The Art of Forgiveness, Lovingkindness and peace*. Bantam.

Brown, B. (2012). *Daring Greatly: How the Courage to be Vulnerable Transforms the Way We Live, Love, Parent, and Lead.* Penguin UK.

Mindfulness. (n.d.) *In Oxford Learner's Dictionaries.* Retrieved from https://www.oxfordlearnersdictionaries.com

Martin, S. (2020, January 24). The Need to Please: The Psychology of People-Pleasing [Blog post]. Retrieved from https://blogs.psychcentral.com/imperfect/2020/01/the-need-to-please-the-psychology-of-people-pleasing/

Taylor, J. (2012) Personal Growth: Your Values, Your Life: Are you living your life in accordance with your values? [Blog post]. Retrieved from https://www.psychologytoday.com/us/blog/the-power-prime/201205/personal-growth-your-values-your-life

Parker, T. (2016). 6 Steps to Mindfully Deal with Difficult Emotions. [Blog post]. Retrieved from https://www.gottman.com/blog/6stepstomindfullydealwithdifficultemotions/

Vilhauer, J. (2018). 3 Effective Visualization Techniques to Change Your Life. [Blog post]. Retrieved from https://www.psychologytoday.com/us/blog/living-forward/201806/3-effective-visualization-techniques-change-your-life

Strauss Cohen, I. (2017). Important Tips on How to Let Go and Free Yourself. [Blog post]. Retrieved from https://www.psychologytoday.com/us/blog/your-emotional-meter/201708/important-tips-how-let-go-and-free-yourself

Ni, P. (2013). Are You Too Nice? 7 Ways to Gain Appreciation & Respect. [Blog post]. Retrieved from https://www.psychologytoday.com/us/blog/communication-success/201309/are-you-too-nice-7-ways-gain-appreciation-respect

Streep, P. (2020). Using Visualization to Calm Yourself and Manage Your Emotions (Even Now). [Blog post]. Retrieved from https://blogs.psychcentral.com/knotted/2020/03/using-visualization-to-calm-yourself-and-manage-your-emotions-even-now/

Stanborough, R.J. (2019) What Are Cognitive Distortions

And How Can You Change These Thinking Patterns? Retrieved from https://www.healthline.com/health/cognitive-distortions#thought-origins

Strauss Cohen, I. (2018) The Search for Your True Self: Important tips on how to know our true desires. [Blog post] Retrieved from https://www.psychologytoday.com/us/blog/your-emotional-meter/201806/the-search-your-true-self

TED (2011, January 3) *The power of vulnerability | Brené Brown.* [Video] Retrieved from YouTube. URL https://www.youtube.com/watch?v=iCvmsMzlF7o

Chesak, J. (2018). The No BS Guide to Protecting Your Emotional Space. *Healthline*. Retrieved from https://www.healthline.com/health/mental-health/set-boundaries#how-to-communicate-and-set-your-boundaries

World Health Organization. (2020). *WHO Constitution*. [Webpage] Retrieved from https://www.who.int/about/who-we-are/constitution

World Health Organization. (2020). *WHO Mental Health*. [Webpage] Retrieved from https://www.who.int/health-topics/mental-health#tab=tab_1

Kendrick, T., & Pilling, S. (January 2012). Common mental health disorders - identification and pathways to care: NICE Clinical Guideline [PDF]. Retrieved from https://www.ncbi.nlm.nih.gov/pmc/articles/PMC3252532/pdf/bjgp62-047.pdf

Lussier, M. (July 2018). *The Impact Psychological Well Being Has on Physical Health*. [Blog post] Retrieved from https://www.unh.edu/healthyunh/blog/psychological-health/2018/07/impact-psychological-well-being-has-physical-health

MacMillan, A. (February 2017). Why Mental Illness Can Fuel Physical Disease. *Time* [Magazine] https://time.com/4679492/depression-anxiety-chronic-disease/

Wilks, D. *The Link Between Mental and Physical Wellbeing.*

[Article] Retrieved from https://www.myhealth1st.com.au/health-hub/articles/the-link-between-mental-health-and-physical-wellbeing/

Harvard Medical School – Healthbeat. *Good balance requires mental and physical fitness*. [Article] Retrieved from https://www.health.harvard.edu/staying-healthy/good-balance-requires-mental-and-physical-fitness

McGonigal, K. (August 2012). Is You Mind Separate From Your Body? How mind-body beliefs shape your choices and influence your health. *Psychology Today*. Retrieved from https://www.psychologytoday.com/us/blog/the-science-willpower/201208/is-your-mind-separate-your-body

Greco, V., & Roger, D. (April 2003). Personalities and Individual Differences: uncertainty, stress, and health. [Web-page] Retrieved from https://www.researchgate.net/publication/223850969_Uncertainty_stress_and_health

Raab, D. (August 2018). Deep Secrets and Inner Child Healing: research shows that being in touch with your inner child is healing. *Psychology Today*. Retrieved from https://www.psychologytoday.com/us/blog/the-empowerment-diary/201808/deep-secrets-and-inner-child-healing

Raypole, C. (June 2020). Finding and Getting to Know Your Inner Child. *Healthline*. Retrieved from https://www.healthline.com/health/inner-child

Goldminz, I. (September 2018). Emotional Reasoning and other Cognitive Distortions. [Blog post] Retrieved from https://medium.com/org-hacking/emotional-reasoning-and-other-cognitive-distortions-b01f5464d891

Lerner, H. (2004). *Fear and Other Uninvited Guests: Tackling the Anxiety, Fear and Shame that keep us from Optimal Living and Loving*. Harper.

TED (February 2004) *Flow, the secret to happiness | Mihaly Csikszentmihalyi*. [Video] Retrieved from TED: Ideas Worth

Spreading. URL https://www.ted.com/talks/mihaly_csikszentmihalyi_flow_the_secret_to_happiness?language=en#t-630037

Spirit of Humanity Forum. *What is resilience? Interview with Dr. Boris Cyrulnik*. [Webpage] Retrieved from https://www.sohforum.org/2020/01/22/what-is-resilience-interview-with-dr-boris-cyrulnik/

Brown, B. (January 2013). *shame v. guilt*. [Blog post] Retrieved from https://brenebrown.com/blog/2013/01/14/shame-v-guilt/

Earl E. Bakken Center for SPIRITUALITY & HEALING. (2016) *Taking Charge of your Health & wellbeing: What is the Mind-Body Connection?* [Webpage] Retrieved from

https://www.takingcharge.csh.umn.edu/what-is-the-mind-body-connection

Danone Nutricia Research. *Gut and Microbiology: The central role of the gut*. [Webpage] Retrieved from https://www.nutriciaresearch.com/gut-and-microbiology/the-central-role-of-the-gut/

Brain Quotes: Inspire & Motivate. *Greatest Tragedies in Life Quotes* [Webpage] Retrieved from http://www.braintrainingtools.org/skills/one-of-the-greatest-tragedies-in-life-is-to-lose-your-own-sense-of-self-and-meaning/

Good Reads. *Quotable Quote: Lao Tzu, Tao Te Ching*. [Webpage] Retrieved from https://www.goodreads.com/quotes/2979-knowing-others-is-intelligence-knowing-yourself-is-true-wisdom-mastering

Evolve with Lou: Empowering You. *As I began to love myself...* . [Webpage] Retrieved from https://evolvewithlou.com/as-i-began-to-love-myself/

Healthline. *Finding and Getting to Know Your Inner Child*. [Webpage] Retrieved from https://www.healthline.com/health/inner-child

Institute Success. *Eckhart Tolle*. [Webpage] Retrieved from https://institutesuccess.com/library/when-you-become-comfortable-with-uncertainty-infinite-possibilities-open-up-in-your-life-eckhart-tolle/

Good Reads. *Quotable Quotes: John Allen Paulos*. [Webpage] Retrieved from https://www.goodreads.com/quotes/504787-uncertainty-is-the-only-certainty-there-is-and-knowing-how

The Tavistok Insistute. *Sigmund Freud*. [Webpage] Retrieved from https://www.tavinstitute.org/news/out-of-your-vulnerabilities-will-come-your-strength-sigmund-freud/

Shaw, M. *Why is comparison the thief of joy and how to stop comparing yourself to others*. [Webpage] Retrieved from https://madeleineshaw.com/why-comparison-is-the-thief-of-joy-and-how-to-stop-comparing-yourself-to-others/

Pass It On. *Quotes: Ralph Waldo Emerson*. [Webpage] Retrieved from https://www.passiton.com/inspirational-quotes/3392-what-lies-behind-us-and-what-lies-before-us

Good Reads. *Quotable Quotes: Carl Gustav Jung*. [Webpage] Retrieved from https://www.goodreads.com/quotes/75948-the-privilege-of-a-lifetime-is-to-become-who-you

Brainy Quotes. *Aristotle Quotes*. [Webpage] Retrieved from https://www.brainyquote.com/quotes/aristotle_138768

PART II

GROWING STRONGER

Mom,
For your infinite patience and compassion,
For always seeing me as the best version of myself,
Thank you,
I love you.

INTRODUCTION

> *"It's not the mountain we conquer, but ourselves."*
>
> — Sir Edmund Hillary

Life has a way of throwing curveballs at us when we least expect it. You've perhaps encountered a few of these yourself, or are dealing with one right now. It can be hard to understand the meaning behind such situations, and as humans, it's normal for us to seek certainty and stability. After all, this is an ingrained evolutionary tool. When these two are removed from our lives or threatened, it's easy to feel down and start thinking that our troubles will never end.

First, I want to run a little thought experiment. Close your eyes and cast your mind back to your childhood. What is one of the earliest memories you remember vividly? Now, move forward and try to recall a situation that upset you but seems trivial now. Why did you feel this way, and how did you react? Can you remember what was going through your mind?

Now, open your eyes and ask yourself: If the younger version of myself was right here, right now, throwing a tantrum, would I engage? Or, would I simply smile and treat it as an occurrence that will come to pass?

If you're like most people, you'll probably adopt the latter reaction.

Why do you think this would be the case? The short answer is quite simple: you've grown. Not just in age but also temperament, strength, and consciousness. I'm here to tell you that whatever it is you're facing right now isn't as much of a mountain as it may seem. Much in the way that your younger self reacted poorly, unable to see his or her problems, you're likely making your current situation more significant than it ought to be.

I'm not saying your problems are trivial—far from it. In fact, your perceived obstacles are of utmost importance, as they may very well be opportunities in the making. Challenges are a gateway to expanding your comfort zone and becoming stronger. And, of course, life is all about growth. Personal development if the main reason our life situations are constantly evolving. Stagnation in comfort isn't really much of a life, is it? No one ever wrote a great story about a character who was happily undisturbed and dispossessed of ambition - not that I know of, at least (utopian fiction set aside!). You might think you'd prefer a life of perpetual ease and comfort, but ask yourself: Will I truly be content if I never have to face another challenge? Will I be satisfied knowing everything has been done for me? Honestly, don't you think that living this way would eventually become unbearable and excruciatingly unfulfilling?

Norms and Conditioning

So, what makes you, you? Why is anyone the way they are? Obviously, the answer to this question is complex. However, one of the fundamental factors that plays a role in piecing the facets of our being is conditioning.

Human beings are social animals. One of the easiest ways for us to move through life and survive is to mimic what we see around us. For example, let's say you land in a foreign country where you don't know much about the culture or customs. What's the first thing you do after getting settled? You look around and see what other people around you are doing. Mimicry is a useful shortcut we've developed within our survival mechanism.

However, mimicry dulls the senses and puts us on autopilot mode. When we aren't aware of our thoughts and actions, we end up leading lives that are far from our truth. Can you think of some things that you're not satisfied with in your life right now? Are you able to recognize the patterns that got you into these situations? We develop conditioned thinking as we grow, learning these patterns involuntarily from our environment. Within the barriers of societal expectations, it is no surprise that some people never come to realize that our making - our entire way or perceiving and experiencing life - has been programmed. They keep living their lives in the same repetitive way, abiding by their same old thoughts, without ever questioning the validity of these.

By picking up this book, you've taken the first step towards changing your life. I'm not saying this book is a cure-all, but I'm going to show you how you can change your thoughts, and how you can unlearn outdated and unhelpful behaviours and thought patterns. In doing so, you will create a pathway to the life YOU want. We cannot control our environment, but we can control ourselves; therein lies our greatest asset. Our beliefs inform all of our actions. Our actions provide results as an indication or update on how our lives are going. So, once you change your thoughts, your life will follow suit.

Alignment

Were you born with certain beliefs and qualities, or have you learned them over time? The effects of nature versus nurture have been debated within the scientific community for centuries (Mcleod, 2007). The conclusion seems to be that while character is key, nurture (or our environment) plays a significant role in who we become, and there isn't a clearly defined line between which factor is more vital.

The most remarkable aspect of this debate is that it is mainly our mindset that determines which factor is more influential. If you believe that your qualities are set in stone and that you cannot change your way of thinking, you'll ensure that nature (what you were born with) informs results. On the other hand, if you believe in change and believe that you can align yourself with who you want to be, you'll draw lessons from your environment and nurture yourself, creating optimal situations for growth.

Our mind is a powerful tool. It needs to be nurtured and handled with care. You can use a knife to prepare delicious food that brings joy to others, or you can use it for harm. It's up to you to align yourself with whom you genuinely want to be, and to use your mind effectively - and wisely - to get you there. The mind's expansibility is in line with this truth on which our universe rests. All of us are part of the same creation, and hence, this truth equally applies to us.

So, what are your goals, and how can you use your mind to pinpoint and achieve your purpose? This is what I'll be showing you in this book. My aim is to support you in your journey by sharing the most helpful tools and insights I've come across along my own voyage. I must warn you, it won't be comfortable - but frankly, if undertaking the discovery of yourself were not sprinkled with challenges and obstacles, there would be no room to grow. Let me say it again: It won't be easy, but nothing worthwhile is. Sir Edmund Hillary could have looked at Mount Everest and decided it was too high. You are the same creation as the brilliant minds you have read about; you just haven't opened yourself to it yet. You are complete, but have yet to tap into your infinite potential.

Throughout these pages, you will note a recurrent referral to the higher self. The higher self is the (often dormant) part of your being that reflects the very best version of yourself. Your life's purpose and potentiality lies within your higher self. While the specifics of every individual's reasons for being might vary, each and everyone attempts their best. This is our deepest truth. I can show you many paths, but ultimately, the journey is yours to take. You already possess everything you need. It's just a matter of tapping into it.

Have you ever misplaced something and began to frantically look for it, only to realize it was right in front of you the whole time? Or found yourself listening to someone speak who made you think about a topic in a completely different way? It's not as if the lost object or different opinion came into existence the moment you discovered them. They were always there; you just weren't looking for them yet.

This book goes hand in hand with *Growing Into You*. It is intended to help you seek out what is right for your life, beyond the veil of societal conditioning. It will guide you in finding out what works best for *you,* helping you listen to your most profound truth and let go of the need for external validation that has become so prevalent in society. If you put what you read here into regular practice, you'll notice yourself moving closer to your higher self. We will abide by the universal law that science has long-established, which states that every action has a reaction. As you consciously move in alignment with your higher self, what you most *need* will present itself to you.

I can guarantee you that you already possess a most complete tool kit to develop solutions and overcome challenges. Through these pages, we will explore these tools and learn to use them correctly and effectively. Your problems won't just up and disappear, and I can assure you that there will be more obstacles on the horizon. However, I hope that by the end of this book you will come to see these challenges as remarkable opportunities, and that you will feel confident to embrace and grow through change and uncertainty.

Time to change your mindset, because you are capable of offering yourself so much more. Let's begin.

9

AWAKENING

"The path of awakening is not about becoming who you are. Rather it is about unbecoming who you are not."

— *Albert Schweitzer*

THE WORD AWAKENING implies having been asleep or naive to the greater possibilities of your life. Don't blame yourself for this. The truth is, most of us live our lives unaware of its full potential. Awakening to your higher self begins with listening to your intuition.

What is your higher self? Briefly, it's your ideal self. The version of you that is the best possible representation of who you are, deeply connected to a greater intelligence. The objective of awakening isn't necessarily to embody this higher self, but to begin to move towards it. Indeed, aiming to become one with your higher self might lead to a streak of ego-driven perfectionism, which will do you no good in the long run.

Now, intuition is the voice of your higher self. Our brains aren't connected just to ourselves. In fact, you can think of your mind as a node in a vast network of intelligence. This theory was first proposed by Dr. Maxwell Maltx in his book, *Psycho Cybernetics* (Maltz & Kennedy, 2002). Dr. Maltz likened the creative process to a sequence of learning through constant feedback.

Feedback comes to us from our environment. For example, if you're driving somewhere and take a wrong turn, you will realise it at some point due to environmental cues. Either your GPS will alert you, or you'll see a traffic sign that indicates you're on the wrong path. Such feedback is subtler when it comes to your goals and vision. There are no physical signposts; all we have is our intuition, intertwined with the outcomes of our decisions.

Concrete outcomes aside, your brain is connected to more considerable intelligence, and this provides us with insight. If you've ever *had a feeling* about something, you've experienced intuition. Scientifically, we don't fully understand where intuition comes from. Could it be our unconscious mind absorbing facts without our conscious mind knowing? Or perhaps it is the product of our minds linking to a larger, universal intelligence. Such questions remain enigmatic.

Either way, there's no denying that intuition exists. It is often the discreet voice that guides and supports us during challenging times. Yet, the thing with intuition is that it is a very subtle voice, especially when we aren't used to listening to it. It is also often mistaken for a logical thought response to our environment. As you awaken to your higher self, you will learn to differentiate between these voices and tap further into your intuition.

Everyone's intuition speaks differently. For the time being, don't worry about trying to pinpoint the differences between these voices every time something comes up. Instead, focus on listening, observing, and learning. Approach the less comfortable aspects as feedback. Remember that discomfort is a potent seed for growth. Intuition feels differently for everyone, so you need to learn how to make it work for you. Absorb all feedback - physical and emotional - and gently observe how it sits within you. This way, you will keep learning what the unique frequency of your intuition sounds and feels like.

The Subconscious Mind

Our mind is divided into our conscious and subconscious. Estimates vary, but most research has indicated that our conscious minds contain far less information than our subconscious. The best way to think of it is to view your mind as one giant iceberg (Ho, 2020). The portion above the water that you can see is your conscious mind. The bulk underneath the water that makes up most of the iceberg is our subconscious.

Why is our mind structured like this? That same question intrigued a researcher named Jean Piaget back in the 1930s.

His theory of cognitive development remains the gold standard for explaining how we learn information as we grow. But before we get to Piaget, it's necessary to understand the roles these two parts play. Your conscious mind is the most easily controlled portion of your brain. You can use it to direct your focus and thoughts in any manner. You can use it to make choices that impact your reaction in the present. You've probably heard the oft-repeated saying to "always remain present."

Well, this is a simplified instruction to remain conscious or within our conscious mind. The conscious mind is small, but it acts as a great filter of information and choices. These choices arrive from your subconscious. This part of your mind is vast and contains a ton of information you've learned over the years. The longer you live, the more developed your subconscious mind is.

The subconscious's job is to make your life as easy as possible. For example, you wake up and brush your teeth. It would be a pretty straining task if you had to learn to do this every day. Thankfully, you were taught a few times, and the action is now automatic. Your subconscious mind is the learning machine.

Contrary to popular belief that we are less likely to learn new things as we grow older, we continue learning throughout our lives without even trying. It's just that when we're younger, we don't exercise choice when it comes to learning. Consider the way people use social media these days. The majority of us will blindly filter through information depending on our pre-conceived beliefs, choosing to view content and news that adheres to our view of the world, ignoring everything that does not support our prior opinions and ideas.

In short, we're choosing to forge beliefs and learn information that supports our existing worldview. As we grow older, our subconscious automates greater portions of information, and it exerts tremendous force over our behavior. If you were to read new information that is contrary to your beliefs, you would notice that you'd feel physically disturbed. It is easier to automate learnt responses than to undo existing ones and learn something anew.

The difficulty lies in undoing, not in learning. This is why change is hard. The irony is that our subconscious mind convinces us that change is unpleasant and unacceptable, but it is actually the only constant we have in this world. It's no wonder so many of us struggle to live satisfying lives. Change is a gamble that is highly uncomfortable, but it remains the only way to move forward into a fulfilling and rewarding existence.

Accepting change begins by using your mind to focus on and greet the information that is presented to you. Let's say you receive excellent news one day, followed by the occurrence of something terrible. From an unbiased perspective, your feelings are determined by what you decide to focus on. Would you be able to remain balanced, taking in both pieces of information and reacting without judgment, therefore without immediately investing yourself emotionally? Truth is, for one thing, you always have the option to direct most of your energy on the good news, and even use the boost of positivity to help deal with the bad. On the other hand, you could also choose to pinpoint and highlight your misfortunes, how low you feel as a result, and ultimately dim the good news. Abiding by a positive or negative standpoint is entirely your decision.

Unfortunately, most people are inclined to direct their

energy towards negativity, and not randomly or by accident. Our brains have a built-in survival instinct (Schoen & Loberg, 2014) that focuses on the negatives more frequently than the positives. This is supremely useful when living in the wild, where life-threatening circumstances and accidents are more likely to occur. However, this isn't beneficial to our modern lifestyles. Instead of wild animals or harsh weather conditions, stress and limiting beliefs present themselves as threats.

By living in a constant state of stress, you're teaching yourself to focus on what's negative. As this becomes automatic, you do it unprompted, and the rest of your life follows suit. So, what is the solution for this? Break the pattern. The first step to doing this is to understand how it is formed in the first place. This is where Jean Piaget, whom we introduced earlier, comes in.

The Theory of Cognitive Development

Piaget's work came about primarily because he vehemently disagreed with the idea that a person's abilities were defined at birth. His research was focused entirely on how children build mental learning models, but given the hold the subconscious has over our lives, it's appropriate for adults as well.

His work was aimed at understanding how children form the most basic ideas. For example, how does a child understand the concept of time or numbers? Piaget developed a cognitive theory in three parts:

- Schemas
- Adaptation processes
- Stages of cognitive development (Mcleod, 2018)

These three parts don't build into each other. Instead, they work together to form a complex web of learning. Schemas are fundamental building blocks of knowledge. Consider them as units of knowledge tucked away in the back of our minds (subconscious). A child adds more units of knowledge in their brains as they grow older and interact with their environment.

The key point here is that children do not have fully developed conscious minds. They store everything directly into their subconscious. You can certainly understand why. Children are taking everything in about this new world they're in, and the conscious mind is an impediment to this process. After all, picking and choosing information to learn isn't very helpful to a child. They have lots to learn and are best served incorporating information as quickly as possible.

Schemas link to one another and define behavior. For example, a child of a certain age might observe their parents ordering food at a restaurant and install different schemas for entering the new space, being seated, looking at the menu, ordering food, waiting, eating, and paying before leaving again. These schemas link to one another to define a behavior called "eating at a restaurant." Schemas can be present in more than one behavioral pattern. For example, the schema that defines paying for a meal can link to a more prominent behavioral pattern or concept regarding money and services.

The formation of behavioral patterns is what Piaget termed adaptation processes. There are three stages to this, as he described it. The first stage is assimilation, the second is accommodation, and the third is equilibration.

Imagine a child looking at a bald man, pointing directly at him, and yelling "clown!". The child has most likely assimilated information about bald heads using schemas and has accommodated it by enacting a behavioral pattern. As for equilibrium, if the feedback the child receives is desirable, he learns that his behavior was correct and installs it deeper into his subconscious. If his mother tells him that the bald man isn't a clown and that he shouldn't shout, it creates disequilibrium. His brain breaks the link between schemas and forms new ones according to the new information received. Questions are asked to form new connections and move towards a state of equilibrium.

So, what should you take away from this? First, you have certain schemas installed deep within your subconscious, which your environment validated and reinforced when you were young. Your environment includes observations, interactions, behaviors, and the people from whom you learned information. It's better to think of your environment as a melting pot of sources of information.

Your environment continually provides you with feedback that moves you into equilibrium or disequilibrium. The problem with adults is that we use our conscious minds to seek equilibrium since disequilibrium is so uncomfortable. I say "problem" because if we repeat this behavior often enough, we embed the schema even more into our subconscious. Instead, we need to break this pattern by reexamining the information that validated our schemas in the first place.

"Money is bad/uncomfortable/not important/scarce." This is a schema that most of us have in one form or another, no matter which part of the world we live in. Most of us possess strong beliefs about money that were validated by our environment when we were growing up. Perhaps the information you received came from your parents. They might have told you that money doesn't grow on trees and that it doesn't come by easily. As an adult, your engrained perception is that money is scarce.

To break this schema or remove it, you need to reexamine the information. This moves you into disequilibrium, which prompts further learning. As an informed adult, you can use your conscious mind to seek out unbiased information, and begin to recreate schemas from a new perspective. Keep acting according to these new arrangements, and the old ones will begin to deactivate themselves.

For example, look at the list of the wealthiest people in the world. Jeff Bezos is at the top with over a trillion dollars. How can money be scarce if one man, a person who is the same as you and me, has that much? It doesn't necessarily come down to opportunity or innovation. Marcus Licinius Crassus was the richest man in ancient Rome. In modern terms, he's thought to have possessed a billion dollars in gold alone. Does his life make it sound as if money is scarce?

We have all been taught certain things, all of which sit within the relative concept of truth. Even so, we don't have to continue believing them just because they make us feel secure. In order to grow past your limiting beliefs, you must face the discomfort of disequilibrium. As you know, you are only as strong as your mindset. Hence, if you willingly choose to greet change with positivity and accept to navigate discomfort, you are more likely to experience personal growth and to observe favorable changes within yourself.

Defining Yourself

Now that you've learned that you have limiting beliefs within you, and more importantly, why these beliefs exist, it's time to face them. Who do you want to be, and what do you want your life to look like? This isn't an easy task. Most of us have been conditioned by external validation and our environments for so long that we don't even know what truly makes us happy.

If you're feeling regret or that there must be more to life than what you're doing right now, it is very likely that this is your higher self calling you. It is an indication that you have it within you to live a life much more fulfilling than the path you are following right now and, in your own way, to live up to your full potential. It might just take time and willingness to remove the veil you've placed over your head.

TO GET where you need to be, you must first determine where you are going. This is why goal setting is crucial. Your goals need to be relevant to who you are. It might take you time to figure out who "you" really are, so don't worry if you make a few wrong turns along the way. Here's a handy framework that can help you better define your goals.

First, I would like to challenge you to attempt to define your purpose. Your purpose is your core spirit. It's what moves you and energizes you like nothing else ever will. For example, some people's purpose in life is to help others realize their dreams or alleviate their burdens. The way they execute this purpose is with a vision. The vision can be volunteering, starting a nonprofit organization, or raising funds for those in need. It could also be something like starting a business that empowers people to become entrepreneurs and achieve their dreams. You can provide services such as social media marketing to small business owners to help increase revenue. Conversely, you might feel entirely fulfilled by living a quiet life, raising healthy children, and caring for your loved ones. There is no right or wrong here, as long as your purpose is what sits perfectly within you.

There are many ways of achieving your purpose, one of

which is your vision. Goals act as waypoints in your vision and inform you about whether you're on track or not. Let's say you're raising money for a charity. With a given timeline, you could easily set goals that measure your progress towards the final amount. Similarly, you can create specific tasks from a set timespan that will help you achieve your goals.

Most people get stuck on far-reaching goals such as "I want to be a millionaire" or "I want to be an entrepreneur." These shouldn't even be considered goals or put in the same category. They are dreams or visions without a purpose, ideas without substance. Your goals should be created in alignment with your purpose - the bigger picture, if you will. Finding your purpose might be a trial and error process at first, so get comfortable with putting yourself first, listening to your gut instinct, questioning the choices you are making, and asking yourself what you truly want.

This might seem intimidating, and that is perfectly normal at the beginning. Remember, you're fighting against decades of established cognitive patterns! Be kind to yourself, start slow, and be willing to work with your internal self rather than against it. Ask yourself what it is you want to do right now. Go ahead and try it now while reading the rest of this section, and see what pops up. Build little victories like this whenever you can. I'm not saying you should go out and do every single thing that comes to mind. Have trust in your intuition to know the difference between something impractical and what will bring you long-term fulfilment.

Here's a reminder. Instead of focusing on the fact that you can't get what you want at a given time, perhaps shift your energy to focus on what you do have and how you can act to improve your situation. You have complete control over your life - not over what happens, but over how you approach and perceive any situation.

So, think about it. What can you do that will bring you real joy and make you feel good about yourself? Take some time to think along these lines. Finding your purpose isn't a destination; it is a journey.

*Avoiding **Self-Sabotage***

Once you begin your journey of finding and living your purpose, your brain will begin to fight back. All of those past schemas might start rebelling out of withdrawal and lack of use. Your subconscious mind will find that you've reduced or suppressed many of the things you usually automate.

Naturally, it's going to try to push you back towards your old patterns, since that is easier; it requires less energy and is a place of comfort and security.

This is where awareness plays a huge role. Monitor your thoughts as much as you can and notice when your subconscious mind tries to push you down your old path. For instance, if your current goal is to cut down on sugar and high-processed food, notice what your mind tells you when you're eating nutritious foods or when you think you feel hungry. Your mind exhibits a pattern, so it's up to you to learn the many ways it will try to trick you into sabotage. Don't get angry or lose patience. Remind yourself of the reasons why you are resisting old habits, and always be kind to yourself.

Why is being kind to yourself so important? The process of awakening is challenging! It requires all of the resources you have at your disposal. You can't function properly if you're constantly berating yourself about how you're screwing up or how you're not able to change. This is just another way your mind tricks you. Instead, by being kind, you can eventually reprogram your brain and break this pattern.

The little efforts and victories that will surface as you begin to change will create a snowball effect. You will need to put in a lot of work to piece your new habits together and align them with your goals and purpose. But before you know it, you will have built momentum and your new ways will sustain themselves. At this point, you won't need to expend as much effort as when you began.

With time, your mind will automate these new ways and begin sustaining your new, healthy habits by itself. This momentum will enable you to build even better habits on top of it and effect change quickly. It takes some work, but I promise the payoff is worth it!

So, what are some of the thoughts and self-sabotaging traps that your mind will likely throw your way? Everyone is different, so I can't tell you exactly what's going to happen. However, here are some typical self-sabotaging statements that the mind likes to throw our way:

- "I'm going to screw this up. It's too good to be true."
- "I don't deserve this."
- "This is way too easy; it can't be real."
- "He/she/they (is) are too good for me."
- I'm overweight/poor/thin/bulky/weak/inflexible/too flexible, etc.

As you begin each day, set your intention to monitor your thoughts. You can do this by writing down and repeating the words, "Today, I will remain aware of my thoughts and notice any self-defeating words I tell myself." As you go about your day, keep checking in with yourself. Notice how you behave in certain situations. When your boss looks at you, do you look away? Do you change your behavior depending on the person you're talking to? Notice and do your best to discontinue negative thought patterns.

If possible, take some time during this day (even five minutes is great!) to be by yourself and visualize how you want to behave in various situations. Visualize achieving your goals and feeling good about yourself. Ask yourself, "How happy will I be when I achieve this vision?" and really *feel* that emotion. Keep your awareness as high as you can throughout your day.

As your day comes to a close, conduct a mental review of how you behaved, spoke, and thought throughout the day. Do a mental replay of some things that happened during your day, and gently observe whether your reactions reflect the person you genuinely are, in view of your values. Then, ask yourself three questions:

- What will I keep doing tomorrow?
- What will I avoid doing or thinking tomorrow?
- What did I do well today, and why was it good?

With some perspective, take a few minutes to replay the not-so-good moments of your day. Can you use your imagination to change the outcome? Next time, how might you react in a similar situation, knowing what is best for yourself?

A lot of self-sabotage occurs because we generally default to talking ourselves down, especially when stressed. Break these old beliefs and rewrite your schemas with kindness. Treat yourself as you would a loved one. In the words of

Roderick Thorp, "We have to learn to be our own best friend because we fall too easily into the trap of being our own worst enemy." Your brain will eventually catch on to the new messages and take over for you. That's when you'll see massive changes begin to occur, changes that can and will sustain themselves for a long time.

10

TRESPASSING SOCIETAL GUIDELINES

> *"The reward for conformity is that everyone likes you but yourself."*
>
> — Rita Mae Brown

You learned in the previous chapter that our environment influences how we think and behave. So, what causes people around us to behave the way they do? What factors go into determining which behavior is "right" and which is "wrong?" The dominant narratives we see these days are influenced by many factors. Chief among them is power, and whoever has the most power tends to dominate the narrative.

In current times where information is so readily available, the traditional power structures that form narratives are being challenged. Take the sharp decline in trust that most people have for the mainstream media these days. This is one way to illuminate another skill for your self-development toolbox.

Awakening and connecting with your higher self is a great accomplishment. Yet, sustaining and nurturing this state is also a life-long venture. You will need to be aware of the unseen forces that are influencing your thought processes. Your subconscious mind is constantly scanning your environment and absorbing information. Anything that agrees with your previously established or dominant schemas is added, and what disagrees with it is mostly filtered out. This is why we so often miss what's right in front of us.

To understand how narratives are shaped, we need to dive into a theory called post-structuralism. It might sound complicated, but really, it's quite simple - and very important. Poststructuralism is a concept that is more than definitions and theory. Follow along to understand how the narratives you're fed are created.

Post-Structuralism

Post-structuralism is the study of how power influences narratives and enforces inequalities. The idea is to challenge these powers and promote more inclusive narratives to present a well-rounded picture.

When you get right down to it, post-structuralism is all about questioning who creates societal norms, information, anecdotes, and what gives them the ability to do so (Drew, 2020). Post-structuralist conversations can become intricate when you start questioning whether the dominant narrative is valid or not.

Maybe you've heard the phrase, "History is written by the victors." Who knows if events truly happened as they are retold? The victors present themselves as the good guys, but what if it was the other way around? Extend this argument to current affairs, and you can see how conspiracy theories on anti-vaccination, birtherism, 9/11 truthers, Flat Earthers, and other seemingly head-scratching movements are born.

Acknowledging these are a way to become aware of how societal narratives are created and, more importantly, how you should challenge them on your journey. You will face many obstacles once you begin to live in accordance with your higher self. Understanding how these obstacles have been created will help you overcome them.

Theory

Post-structuralists generally believe that narratives are created by white, male, heterosexual, middle-class individuals of power, and the majority of the media we consume is affected as a result. For example, until recently, most childrens' stories would always paint a stereotypical picture of its leading characters. A brave male in charge, a subservient woman, and other characters - typically unlike your strong Caucasian leads - as villains or the help. History books presented a picture of events as the victors saw them. People of various targeted ethnic backgrounds were presented as being regularly subjugated, which painted them as inferior.

So, considering this information, you can begin by examining the state of discourse around you. Discourse is a term that refers to the general manner of a discussion. For example, if someone mentions a dog, the conversation around it goes to how cute or friendly they are. If you had a traumatic encounter with a dog at some point in your life, you might bring that up as a standpoint to your discourse.

There are many types of discourses society can have

about one topic. This doesn't mean one is right and another isn't. Post-structuralism isn't about finding the truth, it's about examining the dominant discourse and presenting alternatives for consideration. Ideally, you'll choose the one that has the most verifiable facts backing it. Unfortunately, this is not often how or why we choose to adhere to certain ideas.

The concept of truth is also of particular concern beyond discovering the "real" truth. We must be aware that these ideas present themselves as being right when it might not be the case. Truth, as promoted by dominant discourses, has a massive influence over us. For example, if you grew up in a prominently Christian neighborhood, odds are you or your family maintain Christian beliefs. This goes for all other beliefs as well, such as being told as a child that you hold a designated role within the family unit and living up to that expectation as though it is, in fact, who you are.

Theoretical post-structuralism proposes that truth, in an objective sense, doesn't exist. Basically, there is no single, absolute verity. This is a philosophical topic with many rabbit holes to disappear into, but what you need to keep in mind is figuring out how your environment shapes you. Be aware that everything you hear and see can be a dominant narrative posing as the truth.

If dominant discourses shape truth, then it stands to reason that those who have the power to shape discourses shape the truth. This notion of power is not limited to political or social influencers. Remember that, as a child, the people who hold the most power in our eyes and those we trust most are usually our principal carers. They are the ones we look up to, and they are those from whom we seek validation. We easily identify with the way in which they identify us, and these early attachments also influence and shape our inner narrative.

You might be wondering where I am going with this. Well, think about everything you believe to be true. If you post regularly on social media, why do you do this? If you reject it, why is that? Do you watch the news? Do you adopt specific dietary habits? Why do you make these choices? All of your actions reveal the discourse you're buying into.

When alternative discourses are presented to us, we instinctively recoil away from them and cling even more to our version of the truth. By what is known as the confirmation bias, it is in our nature to seek information that confirms what we already believe to be true. Can you begin to see how factors outside your control can influence your mind?

Our mind is an infallible trickster. Our ignorance of how power shapes narratives can be quite destructive, as it prevents the real you from surfacing. The discourse you've bought into, no matter how popular, has been shaped by someone who has the power to influence and manipulate discourse. No matter which choice you make, you're buying into someone's control. The more you buy-in, the more you're giving up your willingness to change, or at very least, to be your own unique self.

If your objective is to change your life, you can see how this is a problem. Let's have a look at other evolutionary and biological factors at play.

Connection

As humans, we are social animals. Even the deepest introvert requires connection. From an evolutionary perspective, our chances of survival are higher in large numbers. This is why we seek person to person contact and suffer from poor mental health if this part of our lives declines. Scientists have long since discovered that social and emotional pain is equivalent to physical pain (Cook, 2020).

Your desire to connect with those around you must be balanced by staying true to your best self. We tend to admire people who flout societal norms and, by all appearances, don't seek validation of any kind. However, that doesn't mean you should ever compromise who you are. Whether you realize it or not, your desire to fit in can lead you to buy into ideas that don't align with your higher self.

For example, in the U.S. right now, pretty much every dominant discourse is tinged with negativity and an "us versus them" mentality. It's pointless trying to debate who started the argument or who's right and wrong. You have to live in this environment and stay true to yourself. As you begin to unlearn and experience the world from a more open perspective, you might find yourself in direct opposition to these narratives. As you start awakening, you'll find that resolutely clinging to your point of view may not be a beneficial way to approach this situation. That would simply result in your buying into another dominant discourse.

Instead, recognize the forces at play and try to seek a well-rounded picture of all situations in which you find yourself. Most importantly, take the time to focus on yourself and on how your thoughts are influenced. Sit down and ruminate on the actions you take every day and which dominant narratives influence you. Most of them might be pretty innocent and harmless. For example, why do you brush your teeth and wear clothes? You brush your teeth because you've bought into the narrative that this is the way to preserve dental hygiene. You might choose to wear certain clothes to protect yourself from the elements or primarily as a means of self-expression.

Not many of us would argue against these popular discourses. It's also hard to see how they might be damaging your life. However, not all narratives and discourses are harmless. I highlighted the example of money in the previous chapter. That was an example of a belief in scarcity. Another topic of discussion that has gained traction recently is rising inequality. There is a discourse that proposes that the privileged few are hoarding money, and there isn't enough for everyone.

You can see how this discourse meshes well with the limiting belief you already carry. I'm not saying this view is wrong or right; that's not the point. The point is to ask yourself whether this view helps you move closer to your goals and aspirations and connect to your higher self. If you aim to earn more money and provide a better life for your family, buying into this discourse isn't going to help you.

The tragic thing is that we often buy into discourses we don't agree with out of peer pressure. Our need for connection and acceptance causes us to behave in ways that go squarely against our true selves, affecting our life choices and the paths we choose. We often berate teenagers for giving into peer pressure, but the fact is that we are all extremely vulnerable to social pressure throughout our lives.

Perhaps the best example of our need for connection driving us into delusion is social media. We have come to be constantly bombarded with images of people living seemingly flawless lives, captured by one perfectly staged post after another. This pushes us to create and convey an image that isn't true to who we are. We wait hungrily for likes and comments, feeding off of the dopamine rush every time a notification pops up. We make "friends" on these channels and live vicariously through their exploits. We do all of this to enhance the degree of connection we feel. The problem is that these connections aren't genuine, let alone beneficial to our wellbeing.

You need to exercise a lot of awareness to figure out what is real and what isn't in the world of media. Social media can be a great tool to stay in touch with people. However, it can just as easily lead you to make poor life choices. Unfortunately, social media defines many dominant discourses these days.

Constantly evaluate your choices and check whether you're following these discourses voluntarily or mindlessly. How do these choices dictate your life, and how can you snap yourself out of the ones you haven't chosen? Most importantly, how well do the narratives you choose mesh with who you truly are?

Spirituality

Spirituality, in this context, is about getting closer to your most authentic essence. Once you start settling comfortably into yourself, spiritual, philosophical, and intellectual themes converge.

I'd like to encourage you to journey within. Buddhist philosophy reminds us that to master the world, one needs to master oneself. Mohandas Gandhi once echoed this philosophy when he said that to see a change in the world, one needs to be the change themselves. To put it simply, if you want the world to have a certain quality, start by practicing this quality yourself. Our beliefs inform our choices, which in turn inform our actions. To change your results, you need to journey within and alter who you are. Wouldn't it be foolish to expect betterment without having the willingness to change? The good news is, you can grow and evolve past this person by thinking differently and learning to create solutions.

Spirituality and spiritual practices, such as meditation and visualization, won't create finite solutions. Instead, they put you in a better position to create them for yourself. This is the essence of growth. The more connected you become to yourself, the more awareness and solutions you will develop. In doing this, you'll begin to trust who you are, learn to follow your intuition, and lead from a place of authenticity. From another perspective, you'll be installing schemas relating to your increased competence and ability to deal with problems in your life. Remember the snowball effect? Well, the same thing happens here. You build more confidence on top of your existing competence, and so on, making both grow synchronously.

It all starts with quieting your mind, sitting still, and retreating into yourself. Meditation has proven to literally change your brain (Hanson, 2009). Best of all, there is no downside to this practice. Even five minutes spent in contemplation of your breath has been proven to have benefits. Think of it as exercising your awareness. The more you meditate, the more you observe your thoughts and the tricks your mind plays.

Regular practice helps you differentiate between your true self and the part of you that reacts in unhealthy ways to your environment. In some circles, this part of you is called the ego. The ego has some definitive characteristics that make it easy to spot. For starters, the ego is an avid time traveler that likes to live either in the past or the future. It uses the past to create regret and the future to generate anxiety. It builds mountains out of molehills and convinces you that you can never pass them.

The ego is perplexed by the present, which is why its voice is loudest when you sit quietly and observe. This is when the ego starts chiming in because it's accustomed to being in control. It begins to remind you of the things that need to be done, the messages you need to send, the emails you need to respond to, how to respond to them, how to mitigate negative replies, on and on in an endless chain of worry and stress.

Now, stress and anxiety are often confused for one another or even mistaken as being one and the same. So, let's take the time to define them precisely. Stress is a biological response to a perceived threat in a given situation. If your brain determines that a particular situation is threatening to you, it kicks you into a state of stress. This means your heart beats faster, pumps blood to your limbs, and prioritizes certain bodily functions like respiration and directing blood to your muscles, over other functions such as digestion and reproduction.

Anxiety can be viewed as a reaction to prolonged stress, sort of a chain response to a build up of distorted thoughts we create and sustain. More often than not, anxiety is entirely unwarranted. We mustn't forget that some degree of stress is necessary as it keeps us on our toes and makes us more alert and aware of our environment. However, anxiety is a near-chronic state of emotional strain, where the body's stress-response fails to disappear once the stressor is gone. While stress tends to kick in for short periods at a time, anxiety can remain present and has a tendency to spiral out of control. Anxiety usually presents itself as an inner voice and loves to run wild if left untended.

With practice, patience, and the right tools, it is possible to tame anxiety. By learning to observe and simply smile at its voice, you reduce its power. A powerless ego equals a peaceful existence. The present moment is full of possibilities, and meditation teaches you to observe its power. Time doesn't exist in the present. It's always "now", after all.

Naturally, our choices in the present moment define our future. The past cannot be changed, and it no longer exists in the present. At this very moment, you can choose to be whoever you want to be. The past has no hold over you and is somewhat irrelevant. This is a universal truth. Think about everything you've learned so far in this chapter. The discourses you've bought into and the beliefs you've erected in your mind all exist in the past. No rule or law says you have to accept them. You have the power to adopt new beliefs and choose to live according to them from this moment onwards.

It's easy to say this, of course. Your mind isn't going to simply roll over and comply. It will put up a struggle, and you've just learned why this happens. This is where compassion steps in. When people first begin making changes in their lives, they have a ton of enthusiasm that fuels them to carry out the actions that bring them the results they desire. Even so, it is a certainty that obstacles will eventually present themselves.

This is when the old schemas in the brain begin to resurface. You'll feel lazy or unmotivated and begin to create an inner dialogue filled with excuses. We are true champions at convenient self-persuasion and manipulating ourselves! You will convince yourself that you deserve a break, perhaps opt-out of your new habits for some time, and the next thing you know you'll be back into your old routine. At this point, you'll be tempted to feel ashamed or beat yourself up and vow to get back on track. However, fueling yourself with frustration and anger is not a long-term solution. These emotions place your body under immense stress, and no one can function well under these conditions for long.

Instead, be kind and compassionate towards yourself. Your initial enthusiasm is powerful, but understand that it's not going to last. Much like a shot of adrenaline, it'll eventually dissipate, leaving you to confront your challenges and face all that you've buried under those self-destructive habits. Kindness towards yourself and the will to prioritize yourself is what drives change. This is why kindness, compassion, and empathy are such a big deal in ancient Eastern philosophy. It is why you must, first and foremost, fill your own cup with love and compassion.

The Perfection Trap

When you encounter obstacles, are you able to focus on solutions to the problem rather than the obstacle itself?

Let's say you've resolved to workout for at least an hour every day in a chosen physical activity. Your average motivational video on YouTube would tell you to stop being lazy and seize the day, focus on the results, etc. This may pump you up in the moment, but it is not a lasting way to motivate yourself. It works in short bursts, but you can't expect it to fuel you forever.

Instead, develop a routine that you can handle. You don't need to become a workout warrior on day one. Results take time, so be patient and trust the process. Celebrate your small wins! This doesn't mean you give yourself a pass the next day and go back to your old ways. It's about motivating yourself through love and compassion. If you feel tired or don't particularly feel like doing that one routine, ask yourself if you can do something else. Showing up for yourself is a huge step in the right direction. Just show up, every time.

Prove to yourself that you are, in fact, your number one supporter. You will often find that completing the first step can lead you effortlessly into the next one, and so forth.

By simply showing up, you're delivering a strong message to your ego. You're letting it know that you are the one in control, that no matter how much energy, strength, or mental focus you have, you will still be there to attempt your best – and that's a pretty good place to start. Just show up and do your best no matter what happens. This way, if you are unable to complete your workout or whatever it was you had planned, you are unlikely to feel disappointed and frustrated. In this case, quitting is not an option – just show up again tomorrow. Remember that being kind to yourself will help you avoid the traps the ego lays out for you.

You might have heard that consistency is what brings results, and this is true; however, you might be making the mistake of confusing perfection with consistent action. Can we just take a moment to acknowledge that no one is at their best all the time? Consider the case of professional athletes whose full-time job it is to train and prepare for their sport. Even these people, with all their training resources and focus, have bad performances. So how can you expect of yourself to be "perfect" every single time?

The concept of perfection is highly relative, and the need to attain it is a product of our ego. Why would you want to be "perfect" anyway? So that you can bask in the social validation it brings?

Perhaps take a moment to pause here, and define what perfection means to you.

- Is perfection an indicator of success?
- Is it a means to feeling happy and fulfilled?
- How do you deal with not achieving your standards of perfection?

- How is this mindset serving you?
- Are these behaviours beneficial, or harmful?

Imagine for a moment, two artists: one paints for validation from their audience, and the other paints for the sake of it. The first painter is continuously worried about producing the perfect painting. The second one paints from within and strives to achieve their highest vision. Who do you think will be happier at the end of the day? Who is going to experience more profound satisfaction with their work?

This example also highlights how we've warped the definition of success in our societies. We revere those who have a ton of superficial evidence of success—money, cars, fancy clothes, etc. However, what good are these "perfect" things unless they're accompanied by a feeling of grounding and gratitude? Having a billion dollars in the bank isn't going to make you happy all by itself. If gratitude is not yet a habit, you will find yourself constantly dissatisfied, no matter what situation you find yourself in or how much you have.

There is no need to strive for perfection, or rather, what society tells you is perfect. Listen to yourself and practice compassion here. Take action on your goals, and do your best. Don't give yourself a free pass, but also don't yell and scream at yourself either. You don't need these negative emotions to push yourself. You could use them in short bursts, if and when necessary. However, never use them in the long run. You'll only burn yourself out and will fall right back into your undesirable routines.

Take some time to think about what success means to you. A good exercise to carry out is to look at people you admire and see whether they're happy with what they have and who they are. You'd be surprised at the number of people we perceive as "having it all" who are actually discontented with their lives. There are as many unhappy "successful" people as there are "unsuccessful" people (the concept of success is very relative!). Money and fame aren't indicators of anything other than external validation, so don't be misled by them. Remain present in each moment, treat yourself with compassion and encouragement, and you'll slowly deactivate the pull your ego has on you.

11

CHALLENGING YOUR PAST

> *"Do not give your past the power to define your future."*
>
> — Dhiren Prajapati

You have now learned that in order to reach your higher self, you must focus on remaining present. This isn't the easiest thing to do since your ego will time travel and push you either into your past or focus on your future. I'd like to make a distinction at this point between dwelling in the past and challenging it. The former involves experiencing your past emotions and continuously reliving them. Imagine running past events through your mind and reacting to those events as if they're happening right now, altering the scenario time and again. That is what is considered dwelling in the past.

Challenging your past is to adopt an empowering stance. You're not associating with the past directly. Instead, you might examine it as a doctor would examine a patient. Don't mistake this for indifference. You're extremely in tune with what has happened to you but aren't associating with the emotions that were present in your past. Remember, you might be a product of your history, but it's never set in stone or unchangeable. You have the power to choose who you want to be in moving forward.

So why is challenging the past necessary? Simply put, you're the sum of all of your experiences. While reliving the emotions of your past isn't exactly helpful without some semblance of control, examining it and connecting the dots to spot patterns in your life can be extremely powerful. For one thing, it communicates to your subconscious that you're in control. You have the confidence and strength to examine your past with a view to empower, rather than debilitate yourself.

That's a strong message to communicate to your subconscious. Over time, your subconscious mind will rewrite your self-image. You'll go from someone who is a slave to the past to someone empowered by the lessons it has provided. You've started on your path towards your higher self and are living your purpose. Remember that your purpose is a journey, not a destination. The very act of setting your intention to move towards the best version of yourself means that you are living your purpose.

Challenging your past and reprogramming your mind for empowerment and success are not acts of a weak person. To move forward efficiently, you need to learn from your past mistakes without becoming emotionally held hostage by them. Not every event in your past is a mistake. You'll undoubtedly have successes that were products of skill or even luck. You'll have experienced results that were brought about by someone else or something you had no intentional hand in. You might have experienced trauma in your childhood, which you obviously had no control over. These events could be positive or negative.

Set your intention to empower yourself by using the lessons from these events. Most people assume that what happened to them shapes and defines who they are. However, by giving those kinds of thoughts power, you become enslaved by them. In a way, the past provides an explanation as to where you are now and who you've become, but it doesn't need to be in the disempowering way that most people think. You can assume there's nothing to be done and sink lower, allowing yourself to be crushed by the weight of your past. Or, you can draw positive lessons from your past and push yourself higher and further. It's entirely up to you- that's the beauty of life!

So, set your intention to empower yourself. Again, this is as simple as closing your eyes and repeating to yourself that you are in control, you call the shots, and your past has made you stronger and wiser. There are strictly no benefits to pulling yourself down.

The next step is to adopt an approach of equanimity towards your past. Think of it as reading a history textbook in class. Don't fall asleep! I am talking about a process which requires you to remain interested yet detached from your thoughts and emotional responses. Emotions are most useful when observed unbiasedly. This is a skill that can be developed through practising equanimity.

Equanimity is a state of accepting reality as is and merely observing it, without getting drawn into it emotionally or paying particular attention to your thoughts. When you are in this state, you are able to observe everything that is going on around you without getting drawn into the turmoil of those events. Equanimity is not indifference. Indifference implies not caring. In contrast, when you're equanimous, you're compassionate and caring towards yourself.

You can also look at it this way. A child who doesn't get a piece of candy he wants is likely to become upset, disagreeable, or throw a tantrum. As a parent, it would be your job to detect and observe this behavior, correct it, and then offer to soothe it. You would recognize that he is upset, but you could refuse to give him the candy just to stop his outburst. The child cannot see this since he is caught up in the emotional disappointment of not getting what he wants. In a certain way, equanimity is recognizing disappointment (or any other emotion) and remaining content in a neutral state nonetheless.

Remaining undisturbed by external stimuli through nurturing equanimity will help you develop resilience and self-confidence, because equanimity emerges from a place of knowing deep within yourself that you will be alright, no matter what happens.

Examining the Past

Past events have installed themselves at varying degrees of depth. Your childhood experiences are buried deep within you while the events you experienced yesterday are closer to the surface. It is often easier to work backward from the present. What are some of the issues you're dealing with right now? Whether it is low self-esteem, a lack of confidence, or even an inclination to attract emotionally unavailable people into your life, much of our current choices and reactions stem from past experiences.

Don't beat yourself up for facing these issues.

Think of yourself as someone who's asking for feedback. You're trying to figure out the best way to move forward and need advice from your past. Focus on trying to figure out where the self-limiting stories you've been telling yourself originated. Often, you'll find that you will be able to link your experiences to ongoing behavioural responses, one at a time, until you reach the source of the limiting beliefs you've come to regard as pure fact.

Many of your limiting beliefs will have originated during childhood. This can be an issue since it might be tough to recall exact experiences from that point in your life. It might be more helpful to find out what your parents remember and how they reacted during various events that occurred during your childhood. Our parents mean well for the most part, but don't forget that they are only human; ordinary people just doing the best they can. They will have unknowingly installed limiting beliefs within you, without ever realising the chain of events in which this would result.

It might be tempting to get stuck in the past and blame your parents for all of your problems. Our ego loves playing the victim since it derives a sense of identity from this trauma. Identity is the ego's other major obsession, along with time. The ego has a deep-seated need to differentiate itself or define itself in some way. The emotions it uses to determine behavior can be positive or negative. This is why many people who suffer from anxiety, depression, and other unfavorable mental conditions find it hard to overcome these psychological life-depreciating hurdles. Their egos are firmly in control and are using negativity as a means of defining their identities.

Don't fall for this trick. Try to adopt a level approach to face your issues. It will be hard at first to quiet this voice you have nurtured for so long, but continuously remind yourself of the bigger picture and of your higher self, or the person you are beneath it all. Over time, you'll condition yourself to remain on an even keel and will avoid the ego's traps.

*Overcoming **Trauma***

You might have suffered from a particularly traumatic experience during your childhood. It is estimated that over 70% of adults in the United States have experienced some form of trauma in their lives (Bayes-Fleming, 2019), and 20% of these people will go on to experience post-traumatic stress disorder (PTSD) as a result.

Trauma is defined as the emotional experience your brain creates to cope with a disturbing experience. It can be related to a one-time event or caused by ongoing lifestyle situations. As we all respond differently to life events, there is no precise right or wrong in defining what consists of a traumatic experience. There is also a vast array of coping mechanisms we use to protect and shield ourselves from pain and suffering.

It is tough to move on and process trauma in a healthy manner. Traumatic experiences can occur at any point in our lives, but children are particularly vulnerable. Fear is the underlying characteristic of response to trauma. It could manifest through fear of intimacy, of meeting new people, or a fear of being humiliated. These apprehensions color everything you do and define how you experience the world. Going back to the theory of cognitive development you learned in the previous chapter, you can understand how trauma installs fear-based schemas in your mind.

Given its deep roots and painful consequences, trauma is best handled by first accepting that you are affected by it. Like with everything else, acceptance is the first step to finding peace. Next, it's best to seek help from a professional; either a therapist or psychologist can be of great use to you. Unfortunately, there's still some stigma in our society that connects seeking help to declining mental health. Don't make the mistake of undermining yourself and thinking you should deal with your trauma by yourself; reaching out for assistance requires enormous strength. If you are recovering from traumatic events, seeking out support is one of the bravest and most meaningful actions you can take. Reaching out to someone for help when you're vulnerable is a significant show of strength, just like finishing a marathon with a sprained ankle. By accepting who you are and opening yourself up to another person, you are allowing yourself to begin a healing and recovery process.

Secondly, you'll find much evidence to show that mindfulness and meditation help immensely in recovering from trauma. Research has shown that meditation can help trauma victims better deal with their issues (Bayes-Fleming, 2019). Note that meditation by itself is a means of becoming aware of what's going on in your mind. You'll still need to take action to overcome your issues and implement positive habits that will install new schemas in your mind.

Here's a simple meditation technique that you can practice every day. All you need is five minutes and a place where you won't be disturbed. Begin by sitting down on the floor or a chair. Make sure your back is free to take shape without support. Take a few deep breaths and slowly close your eyes if this is helpful. Observe your breath. Notice the nature of your breath without modifying it. Notice how you inhale cool air and exhale warm air.

Notice which nostril you're exhaling and inhaling from. Are both nostrils open or just one? Now, move outward and scan your body. Notice the sensations in it. Merely observe them and don't dwell for long. Keep scanning your body, from the top of your head to the tip of your toes, until you've covered all of it. You can then perform another scan or merely become aware of your environment. Listen to the sounds in your environment; notice them without judgment. Just listen and observe.

Close out your meditation by setting a short-term intention. What are you trying to overcome at the moment? Every day brings its lot of ups and downs. How will you greet these unpredictable tides today? Will you choose to react or observe as they flow through? Before you check-out, make a mental note to keep being kind towards yourself and treat yourself with the utmost importance.

Overcoming trauma is not something you can do overnight, by any means. However, with consistent work, willingness, and a positive attitude, you'll overcome your issues. Set your intention to prioritize yourself above all else, and begin your journey. Do your best to learn from your past instead of becoming emotionally involved with it. You might not get it right the first or maybe even the 10th time. That's OK! What's important is that you keep working towards staying connected to your higher self and keep moving further away from the hold that your past experiences have over you.

The Limbic System

Stopping yourself from becoming emotionally involved with your past is easier said than done. Why is this? Why does your brain want to live continuously in the past? The previous chapter gave you psychological insight into why this is the case. However, the reasons for your brain behaving this way aren't just psychological. There's a physical reason as well.

Our bodies are partly composed of a high functioning nervous system. This nervous system is made up of tiny nerves that process input from our environment and delivers it to our brain. Your brain will attempt to make sense of the inputs through the prism of your schemas, and direct messages to your nerves with regard to how your limbs and body ought to react. The nerves deliver these messages, which enables you to react to environmental stimuli.

A big part of your nervous system is the limbic system. The limbic system is buried deep within the brain, below the cerebral cortex, and above the brainstem (*The limbic system*, 2019). The primary functions of the limbic system involve learning, memory, emotion, and motivation.

Now, here's how your brain physically stores information. When I spoke of schemas in the previous chapter, you might have thought of your brain as being a large filing cabinet. However, this is not the case. Your brain stores information in a radial pattern using neurons.

Neurons are brain cells, and they have the ability to connect and form networks. Each neuron can be a part of multiple networks, just like a schema can be a part of numerous adaptation processes. Neurons form neural networks, and it is these networks that are dialed up when you experience stimuli from your environment. Your brain lights up when a neural network is called into action.

The amazing thing with neural networks is that they get stronger the more often they're used. For example, your "brushing my teeth" neural network is pretty strong since you use it every day. Similarly, the neural networks that formed your limited self-belief are also strong since you've been strengthening them for a long time. Rewiring these networks takes constant practice, strong intention, and directed focus.

In addition to setting your intention and constantly repeating actions, emotions play a huge role. Feelings have been proven to deeply embed experiences into our brains, and they help create stronger neural networks (Hanson, 2009) - for better or worse. We are often able to recall minute details from our past by associating things to events that generated an emotional response within us. Therefore, if you intend to change your behavior, you need to repeat the desired action with as strong an emotional and meaningful connection as possible.

The power of emotions is also why trauma buries itself deeply into our minds. The negativity that trauma brings is a powerful force when it comes to creating strong neural networks. This is why strong emotions often resurface when we visualize certain past events. To rewire the past's hold over you, you'll need to break old patterns by creating new neural networks.

This is why examining the past in a detached manner and injecting your new habits with a healthy dose of positive emotion is so powerful. It is also why you shouldn't remain emotionally attached to your past, a toxic pattern that reinforces those negative neural networks in your brain. You can pause now and choose to put an end to the vicious circle, and refuse to dwell on what was or what might have been.

Conversely, I encourage you to attempt to observe your past from a detached point of view, as you would while watching a movie detailing someone else's life story. It might evoke some sentiment, but it does not belong to you - you do not have the power to alter it, nor is it your burden to carry. The choice to return to the present moment is always yours.

. . .

Techniques

Injecting emotion with focus and intention sounds a bit complicated, doesn't it? How are you supposed to do all of this exactly? Well, it is actually much simpler than it sounds. It begins with your brain and the limbic system, which have the ability to feel emotions tied to the pictures running through your mind. While asleep, these pictures can appear as a blend of the past, or sometimes the dreaded future.

Why not use this ability to your advantage? Why not visualize the desired future and feel those emotions instead of torturing yourself with the undesirable past? I touched briefly upon visualization in a previous chapter. Most people think visualization requires a lot of effort and that they need to learn different techniques or something else entirely. The truth is, you're already an expert at visualization. It's just that you've become accustomed to visualizing the worst-case scenarios for everything in your life.

You have the ability to visualize the positive and to turn it into a real experience. It's a skill that you need to teach your brain. Visualize your goals and ask yourself how you would feel once you become the person you deserve to be. Feel the positivity flow through you as you do this and indulge in the picture. Your brain tends to seek information that supports its world view. This is considered as the confirmation bias, and you can use it here to your advantage. The more you build a picture, the more your brain will seek evidence that supports this new image.

It's vital for you to feel the emotions associated with this pleasant experience. Your brain isn't going to remember the pictures exactly as they are, but it will certainly register the emotions. By focusing on the emotions instead of the details, you'll allow your brain to associate the positive emotion with other similar images in your present life. For example, let's say you visualize yourself lying on the sand on some Hawaiian beach, sipping a drink with a little straw umbrella. You feel the sunshine and hear the waves beating against the shore. The sky is blue, and the water is pristinely clear.

If you happen to find yourself on a beach in some other place, where the sky isn't as blue, and the water isn't as inviting, does this mean you won't feel the positivity? If you invest all of your energy into creating that perfect Hawaiian beach each time, you're limiting yourself to feeling good only in those exact conditions. Instead, take a moment to focus on the emotion. Let yourself be submerged by the warmth, peace, and security this brings. You can carry this emotional and mental state with you. Allow your brain to hear the waves beating against the shore and feel the elements of the beach, even when you're out in the open. It'll automatically dial-up those positive emotions, and you'll feel good.

While it's essential to be specific with the details of your visualization, do so with the aim of making the picture appear real. Don't limit yourself to only that picture or think that you'll feel great only if everything in that picture is met. That's another trap your ego lays for you. By requiring every detail to be satisfied in real life, your ego is just creating an identity for itself. It's creating one that says, "I am happy only in these specific conditions." Obviously, that's not your intention.

By feeling the emotions and focusing on the positivity, you'll make it much easier for yourself to associate with them in the moment. If you're unaccustomed to meditative activities, it might take a great deal of effort to close your eyes and visualize a specific picture. It's far easier to break it down by "feeling" an emotion, by associating little details connected to it. As you get better at visualization, you'll be able to dial those positive emotions without batting an eyelid. You'll be able to summon it in the background as you go about your day, and you'll find your brain assisting you in this endeavor.

This is because the neural networks associated with your self-image will shift towards one that says, "I'm a happy person." This is what we're after at the end of the day. Who cares how happiness comes and in what form it presents itself? In the end, how beneficial it is to your wellbeing is the only thing that matters. So, sit back, visualize, and allow yourself to feel happiness. Know that it is accessible. Understand that happiness is not something to be earned but a state to be chosen. You'll soon feel it as true.

Another technique you can use is positive affirmations. Like visualization, many people inadvertently misuse affirmations. They write positive statements that are future-based, recite them in front of a mirror, close their eyes, and say it like a wish. For starters, your words should be framed in the present. A counterexample would be, "I will get into shape and weigh xx lbs." It is an end goal with no substance which leads your mind to focus on your current state and deceptions. This is ineffective. Instead, you might try "I am strong and healthy, and I will continue to improve my fitness and health". This latter statement is so much more powerful. Phrase your intention in a way that shows you already have what you want.

Note that your statement should only ever be phrased in a positive manner, avoiding negativity and pessimism.

For example, "I will eat healthy food three times a day" is a better statement than "I will not eat junk food all day." Your brain cannot process the negative message and will ignore the "not eat" portion of the statement, thereby reinforcing the unhealthy habit.

Again, this is not wishful thinking. It is more of a way to touch base with yourself and acknowledge what you already have – aka, expressing gratitude. In doing this, you are creating space for more of what you want and need to invite itself into your life. This is important, as we so often fail to give ourselves credit for how well we are truly doing and the small things we accomplish each day. If we fail to notice what we are doing right each day, everything we achieve, small or big, will continue to feel unsatisfactory.

Another thing to note is that your brain doesn't understand the concept of time. Time is something the ego is obsessed with. Your brain lives only in the present since it can only react to what's in front of it. This is why it cannot differentiate between a visualized picture and a real one. It simply assumes everything is happening now. This is also why it's possible for you to lose yourself in the moment and lose track of time. It is also why you can feel time stretch interminably when your brain isn't engaged in something stimulating.

When reciting your affirmations, make sure you feel the positivity that the statement brings you. For example, if you say, "I am in shape, and it is like me/feels amazing to workout X times per week," feel the positivity of that statement within you. Notice how it feels to be this person, and start taking small steps – just show up! – and begin to embody what you want.

The best times to practice affirmations are right after you wake up and right before you go to sleep at night. During these times, your conscious mind is dimmed and isn't fully awake. Your subconscious mind is wide open and is ready to accept everything you feed it, without the conscious mind filtering information or imposing doubt. Every statement or visualization you practice at this time, with positive emotion, will install itself deeper into your mind.

So, how long do these practices take to bear fruit?

Research indicates it takes 90 days for your brain to form new neural networks and to constantly start firing them into action (Hanson, 2009). However, it isn't as if everything becomes automatic after this timeframe passes. You still need to practice your new behaviors repeatedly and break old patterns as they arise. Old habits die hard – really hard – and that's a fact. It will be challenging at first, but remember that your mind works like a snowball rolling downhill. As time goes on, change becomes easier to sustain, and you'll slowly but surely build the life you deserve.

Social Boundaries and Authenticity

As you begin moving towards your higher self, you'll find yourself coming into conflict with your existing environment. As you grow, you'll naturally seek out places that suit your new, elevated mindset. You will likely find your current environment at odds with who you are. Most people get frustrated and take this as a sign of a lack of change. They grow impatient and want their environments to change right now and begin trying to force it.

This is a lot like fueling yourself with resentment or anger, or any negative emotion you can think of. It's possible to achieve change this way, but the change you manifest will likely be undesirable. Instead of growing frustrated, try simply relaxing in your environment. A change will come, but even more important than change is that you remain as happy as you can be in your existing environment.

Remind yourself that you'll find yourself at your destination at some point. So, in the meantime, take action and keep repeating your new habits. Enjoy and appreciate your unique journey. Accept that you might get upset at your current environment or circumstances, and understand that this is fine. You're only human, after all. Be kind to yourself and those around you. You are exactly where you need to be, and there is no point in idealizing a different outcome: a need to control your environment and circumstances. Letting go of what you think must be is essential to staying grounded and having a sense of fulfillment. Witness your thoughts from an observer's perspective, without judgment. Allow yourself to flow through the ups and downs, and greet challenges as opportunities to learn and grow.

This is what it means to "be yourself." Your challenge isn't to vault yourself into some imaginary stratosphere immediately. Instead, it's to keep taking regular action and overcome obstacles with love and happiness. Accept that your environment will never be perfect and that social norms and expectations will impede your progress. You have a choice to either react in frustration or to use these challenges to fuel yourself higher.

Choice is ultimately the only power you have. You are free to choose how you react to all situations in your life. Your ego will attempt to confuse you and present situations that seemingly offer few choices or limited options. Imagine someone makes fun of your new habits, and your ego tells you to react with frustration and prove you're better than them. You can choose to react that way or decide to walk away; it's your call. You can also decide to smile and be compassionate. You could explain your actions to this person or hold back. It's entirely up to you because you own you! You really are only accountable to yourself. Exercise your choices well and in accordance with who you want to become.

Also, keep this in mind: another way in which your environment might derail you is by throwing negative information your way. You might read the news and become convinced that everything is a dumpster fire and that there is a lot of injustice in the world. Some days it feels like everyone just revels in complacency and negativity! The truth is much more balanced than what we hear and what we are taught to believe. Choose wisely what you consume - in all aspects - and how you nurture your mind.

The world is as it needs to be for you to become a greater version of yourself, so be thankful for it. Be grateful for the obstacles the people around you erect. They are helping you become more authentic. Relax into the world and keep moving forward!

12

STANDING OUT

> *"Belonging is being accepted for you. Fitting in is being accepted for being like everyone else."*
>
> — Dr. Brené Brown

Here's an absolute truth about our world that might seem harsh at first sight: It is unequal. People are born into it with varying degrees of comfort, resources, and opportunities. Some of us are lucky enough to have been born into relative comfort. Others are born in literal warzones and have to figure out how to lead their lives. Some people are born with unique physical or mental characteristics, which often leads to them being treated differently by the world, and struggling to navigate a system designed for mainstream conventionality.

Ethnicity, sex, religion, economic status, language, caste, creed; whichever factor you associate with can lead to the world knocking you down and denying you opportunities. As I said, it may sound bleak, but the idea is to show you that despite all of this, the world is perfect. It is exactly as it needs to be to help you get to where you need to go.

You have a choice when it comes to believing what you want about the world and its condition. War, disease, and famine are far from good things. It's very easy to give in to a survival bias and look only at the negatives. This is what most people end up doing, and it's why popular media is full of negativity and fear. The media merely gives people what they want. However, you hold the power to exercise your choice and to view the world from a balanced perspective.

The inequality that exists in the world can create false ideas. You've already learned about the post-structuralist view of the world that seeks to create a more rounded view of reality. You may have adopted false identities and truths about yourself due to your sex, ethnicity, or any other qualities that you were born with.

Privilege exists within a very narrow band in our world, so it's more likely than not that you've adopted negative beliefs about yourself. For example, if you're a woman, you've probably become conditioned to think of yourself as weak or overly emotional. Perhaps your cultural background has you conditioned to believe that opportunities will be limited because of your skin color or the language you speak. Your upbringing and socioeconomic status as a young person might have led you to assume the identity of a hard-working person who never has time to relax and has to work twice as hard for everything.

It's perfectly normal and understandable to complain against these seemingly unjust circumstances once in a while. However, assuming that they are your reality would be a fallacy. I'm not saying that the conditions aren't what they are. It's just that the negative emotions that these conditions generate are a product of your reasoning. For example, let's say you feel that the color of your skin makes you face discrimination in society. There is no denying that this situation is your reality. However, letting it define your outlook on the world and dictate how you live your life is your own doing. You can choose not to let your negative emotions form a world view and forge your personal identity.

Many of us feel a massive need to establish an identity. An identity helps us make sense of the world because we can use it to define ourselves. The problem occurs when we let our egos take over. This is when we begin to create identities in every possible situation and stirs away from our authenticity and higher self. Eastern spirituality poses the alternative, indicating that identities are a form of desire, prone to create suffering in our lives. It is said that truly enlightened people let go of their need to define themselves through a constructed identity.

Have you ever tried working towards letting go of the need for an "I" in your life? Turning towards others and teaching yourself to be selfless? Offering the best of ourselves through kindness, empathy, and compassion enhances our wellbeing. And get this: the more grounded and complete you feel, the more inclined you will be to give back. Once we stop worrying about ourselves so much, about our misfortunes and the happenings of our own existence, we realize how irrelevant most of our destructive thoughts and behaviors truly are.

In the meantime, try to find a balance between defining yourself to better live your life and grounding into a state of equanimity, where you can offer more than you take. Recognize when the ego traps you into thinking of yourself in a particular image, one that is almost always informed by input from your environment.

You have no control over the situation in which you were born, and therefore, it makes no sense for you to view yourself as being stuck there for the rest of your life. As I said before, you always have a choice.

Choice and Social Obstacles

Inequality, discrimination, and other social maladies are a part of the world we live in. As much as we would love to get rid of them, the fact is that they exist, and we need to deal with them. How can you live in such a world and still maintain your positivity? Recognizing the truth about polarity in this world is the place to begin. Everything has a polarity to it. The thing about polarity is that one side of the equation cannot exist without the other. Darkness cannot exist without light, and good cannot exist without bad. Think of these polarities as being two sides of the same coin. You have a choice when considering this. You can look at just one side of the coin, or you can contemplate its contradictions as a whole.

In our societies, we, unfortunately, only look at one side of the coin. Nowhere is this more evident than in politics and social discourse. Everyone likes to yell at one another and post intelligent-sounding tweets in an effort to embarrass or humiliate the opposing side. These people think they're very different from one another, but all of them belong to the same side; the negative one. All they allow themselves to see are the opposing party's lesser aspects and only positives on their own side. Such worldviews can only result in anxiety and outrage that serves no one.

It is very easy to look only at the negatives of our situation and focus only on the unfortunate consequences of the life we were born into. However, to move closer to our higher selves, we must look at the bigger picture. Look at the entire coin, if you will. Looking at just the positive side of the coin isn't a balanced and healthy approach either. It'll lead you to live in delusion, and that's not something anyone wants.

Recognize the polarity of the situation in which you are. For example, if you feel you're being discriminated against because you're a woman, recognize that while this is a bad situation, it does not represent society as a whole. Nor does it represent the truth about your life. If you feel this has always happened to you, it's probably because you've been focusing on the wrong side of the coin. Is it really possible that every single human being on the planet is biased against women advancing in society? It seems unlikely, doesn't it?

This is where exercising your willpower and right to choose is essential. You have the choice to step back and away from the situation you're in. Recognize the negatives but don't give them permission to affect your state of mind. Change isn't brought about by railing against the negatives. It's brought about by remaining optimistic about your ability to affect change. You can't stay positive when you're solely focused on what's wrong with the situation. You need to grow past it and create solutions.

These solutions come from a place of creativity and intuition. You cannot tap into your intuition if you're constantly stressed and tired out from thinking about all that is wrong, all the time. It takes a lot of practice, but stepping back and away from problems is the best way to preserve your natural creativity and bring about real change. Allowing yourself to move away from what is not serving you is of significant service to your wellbeing. You will learn to see how equanimity enables us to remain non-judgmental and connect with our deeper, true selves.

Once you begin doing this, you'll recognize that inequalities exist for a reason. Much like how you need obstacles and mistakes to grow, the world needs these inequalities to evolve. The historical record shows that it's been working to develop into something better. Reading current news might not convince you of this, but it's a fact that our world has never been better in its history.

I experienced this first-hand during my travels around the world. When I was traveling through Central and South America, I mostly stayed in random people's homes. I found these people through a travelers' community on the web. My friends and family were always worried about me being in danger and were extremely apprehensive of all of the "bad people" out there. Mainstream media conditions us to believe that all strangers intend to harm us and that we must be wary of all others. This disempowers us, individually and as a collective. Fear is a means of controlling masses. It undoubtedly plays with our minds and turns us into sheep.

On my journey, even though I encountered some sketchy individuals and had my share of bad luck, I trusted the process, believing in humanity, and I was astonished at the kindness I found in complete strangers. Believe it or not, I lived to recount my adventures as living proof that not everyone was, in fact, out to get me. I honestly believe that when you break away from media propaganda and step out into the real world, it is easy to find an abundance of kindness and more good humans than bad ones.

We now live in a world where technology that a person could not have dreamed of as recently as 1980 exists today. We can communicate with one another at the touch of a screen, and all we need is a handheld device and a connection. Over the past century, women have made giant leaps in terms of equality and recognition in society. With more women joining the workplace and breaking barriers, it's no wonder that society's output has increased so dramatically.

Despite lingering problems, ethnic minorities have also made huge advances. Discrimination is lesser than it was a century ago. Themes such as equality, kindness, and social justice dominate public discourse. We're at a stage where the gladiatorial pastimes of the ancient Romans make no sense to us anymore. Can you think of anyone who would derive pleasure at watching people torn apart by wild animals in arenas? Hopefully not.

The world is evolving into something better, and the inequalities that you perceive will help it get there. I'm not saying that our current world is perfect. There are many inequalities that we continue to perpetuate and injustices we carry out in nature and on animals. However, the world is evolving. What's more, everything is precisely as it needs to be for you to achieve your goals and feel complete. It is only when you rise past your self-imposed limits and continue working towards your best self that the world around you improves as well. After all, you're a part of this world like everyone else. What kind of energy are you putting out there?

Are you emitting positive energy and delivering a message of hope and betterment? Or are you continually griping about how everything is wrong and that things need to change? Who would you rather be? Mind you; I'm not asking you to accept injustice. By all means, fight for what you believe in and strive to achieve your goals.

Once again, it's your choice. Exercise it well!

The Growth Mindset

The negatives in the world can get you to believe in the wrong things. You might look at the state of affairs and think that the qualities you were born with, that you cannot be blamed for, will forever determine where you end up in life. It isn't just societal inequalities that can cause you to adopt such a mindset. Things such as intelligence, looks, and physical gifts can also limit you.

If you believe that what you're born with defines you for the rest of your life, then it's pretty obvious which side of the *nature versus nurture* debate you're adhering to. You've already learned that while nature is important, our environment does play a dominant role in determining how we become. This fact alone should indicate that believing in your limitations or that you're somehow "fixed" is incorrect.

The fixed mindset is alarmingly prevalent in our societies. How often have you seen people from wealthy families or famous families treated differently? The very fact that discrimination exists points to how powerful the attraction of the fixed mindset is. The opposite of the fixed mindset is the growth mindset. This term was coined by Carol Dweck, a psychologist and Professor of Psychology at Stanford University.

Dweck is famous for her book Mindset, in which she dissects the origins of the fixed mindset and how it's completely false (Dweck, 2016). She insists that the growth mindset, which supports that our traits can be enhanced throughout our lifetime, is what leads us to success. Repetition and hard work are what Dweck thinks guarantee success. While talent is essential, it only makes a marginal difference at the highest level. To get there, you still have to work hard and cannot coast by solely relying on that with which you are born.

As you're about to discover, there is a more profound argument behind the growth mindset's effectiveness. It has to do with the power of self-image.

Self-Image

Our self-image is the sum of all the thoughts and feelings that hold to be true about ourselves. "I'm a morning person," "I'm a night owl," etc., are some examples of statements that we often tell ourselves. Of course, we're liable to tell ourselves far more harmful things as well. A fixed mindset harms our self-image because it places a premium on our limitations instead of our potential.

This is because a fixed mindset claims that our abilities are set in stone. For example, you might believe you didn't inherit an "artistic gene" that would allow you to draw well. Perhaps you've never even tried to improve your skills! However, sketching is something that can be learned through practice. You can become a good artist through dedication and perseverance.

If you cannot increase your creativity in life, you're going to evaluate opportunities based on how far outside your comfort zone they are. If your willingness to develop creativity is at six out of 10 and an opportunity is at a nine, you're not going to attempt it. You'll be acutely aware of how limited you are. What's more, the knowledge of these limitations is going to define your self-image.

If you're going to walk around only conscious of how limited you make yourself out to be, it'll be hard for you to see how you can live a fulfilling life. You'll likely face no obstacles for lack of challenging yourself but will be miserable nonetheless. Obstacles won't present themselves because you'll never stretch beyond what you think you can safely achieve. Thus, a fixed mindset will have you moving backward. Insecurity and negativity are direct results of such a life, and your self-image will take quite a battering.

Belief in a fixed mindset also makes you very sensitive to external validation. After all, if you're focused solely on your limitations, you're going to seek positivity from the outside. This means your results will be the only source of validation you can have. Guess what happens when you invest all your energy into your results? Perfectionism and self-criticism take hold, and you'll hardly ever manage to feel satisfied with what you do complete, which ironically diminishes what little recognition you can draw from the outside world.

The growth mindset, on the other hand, helps you focus on the process instead of the result.

Processes and Learning

There is no doubt that results are important. However, if you recall the goal-setting framework we spoke of earlier, you will realize vision is the path that fulfills your purpose, and goals measure your progress along the way. To get to those goals, you need to execute your vision. You can't make progress if you stand still, worrying about how far away the goal is. Your vision should contain a combination of the steps you will take along your path, as well as the destination itself. Put something to execution – take action! Make mistakes and learn from them as you move forward.

The fixed mindset doesn't allow for the making of mistakes or learning. After all, if your abilities are fixed, then where does the possibility of making a mistake enter? This flies against the research I highlighted earlier by Dr. Maxwell Maltz. Mistakes are feedback that we receive from our environment. Without them, it's impossible to make progress.

A growth mindset puts a priority on learning new processes and overcoming obstacles. A person with a growth mindset has a healthy self-image that frames them as someone who can overcome all obstacles thrown their way. Abide by a growth mindset, and you'll be surprised at how quickly you manage to reframe your problems and grow past them.

After all, if you believe that all it takes to overcome problems is learning a new process, you'll be willing to face your challenges and dive into learning quickly. Your mind isn't going to be focused on the negatives or how much you don't know. By placing your focus squarely on what you need to do, one small step at a time, you redirect the energy from what you don't know or what you don't have to all the dormant potential that lies ahead.

The growth mindset also emphasizes that success isn't about luck or having an exceptional talent you were born with. Instead, it's a process that involves taking action, incorporating feedback, and continuing to work until you reach your goal. When viewed in this manner, success becomes a matter of time, and it isn't considered a mythical destination you need to magic your way into.

Start Now

Action is the key to success. Many people read self-improvement books and get caught up in debating the philosophy highlighted in them. It's easy to fall into this trap as well. I'm not saying that you shouldn't discuss or contemplate the information you read. It's just that the majority of your time should be spent in action, not in contemplation.

Taking action is both easy and challenging at the same time. This is because we tend to project our fears and past experiences onto the future and envision all kinds of negative outcomes. The prospect of these outcomes activates our ego, and it promptly discourages us from moving forward. It feels far more comfortable relaxing back into our comfort zones instead of pushing our boundaries and exploring how much we can grow.

The key to ensuring you always take action is to remain present. Don't run away into the future or the past. Figure out your best course of action, and then develop a list of tasks to execute. If making a list sounds too much or too scary, create just one task for yourself to take on. Once you've created this task for yourself, go ahead and do as much of it as you can. Simply show up and put one foot in front of the other. That's all it takes to achieve success.

For example, let's say you decide to go to the gym regularly. Your ego might intervene and tell you that you could get injured when working out, or that you might look funny, or that people in the gym will notice how out of shape you are, and so on. Notice how identity-driven all of these fears are. It places the focus solely on your own qualities and what you currently have within you. None of these fears have anything to do with executing a process poorly.

A fixed mindset drives the ego, and being aware of the telltale signs of the fixed mindset is helpful in removing yourself from the ego's grip. Ask yourself what you need to do to get to the gym. You need to change into your workout clothes, travel to the gym, and start warming up. At the very least, focus on changing into your workout clothes. Next, get in your car and drive to the gym. Take it one step at a time – just show up!

When at the gym, you might not feel like working out right away. Put some good music on, start your first routine and see how you feel after. More often than not, you'll see that getting through your workout when you feel lazy like this is relatively easy. You'll learn to differentiate between the signs of your body telling you it's tired versus the mental patterns making you want to give up.

The starting point, where you are today, is the only thing that is fixed. The present moment is all that you possess and all you need to take action and start creating a new life for yourself. The endpoint isn't fixed. All possibilities are available to you, and it depends on how consistently you take action. Show up every day and do something. Even the smallest act can have enormous consequences. There is no such thing as an inconsequential action.

The great thing about the ending point is that it's entirely up to you. You're the only one who can choose and control where you end up. So, plot your way forward according to your vision and set your goals accordingly. Take consistent action and whenever your ego interferes, remind yourself of the growth mindset's principles. Anything can be mastered with enough focus, dedication, and work.

13

LIVING UP TO YOUR POTENTIAL

> It's not the mountain we conquer, but ourselves.
>
> — *Charlie Wardle*

HAVE you ever felt that there must be more to life than what you're living right now? You might have looked into your past as you read through the previous chapters and realized that a gap exists somewhere. You have a lot of potential, but you might feel as though you haven't quite lived up to your full capabilities. Is there a gap between where you currently are and where you belong? Why does this gap exist, and what can you do to bridge it?

The details behind the existence of the gap will vary from one person to another. However, the broad reason behind it is the same no matter who you are: You haven't been focusing on the right things in your life. We go off-track in our lives for many reasons. Sometimes, we don't believe enough in our abilities. Other times, we try to do too much too soon due to impatience and a lack of faith in our process.

The need for instant gratification or results is a good indicator of a lack of focus in your life. Back in the 1960s, Stanford University psychologist Walter Mischel conducted the Marshmallow Experiment (Mischel, 2014). Like with many scientific findings, Mischel set out to study one thing and ended up finding something else; something far more interesting.

Mischel specialized in child psychology and wanted to measure self-control in children. Here's how his experiment was set up. A child five to seven years old was led into a room and sat at a table. A treat, either a snack or a toy, was placed in front of them. They were then told that they could either enjoy the treat right now or wait for 15 minutes and receive an additional one. Which option would the child choose? This is what Mischel and his team observed from behind a screen.

Some children immediately began enjoying their treat while others held on for the full 15 minutes. Mischel observed that some kids literally sat on their hands or deliberately looked away from the treat to avoid temptation. In some cases, kids were willing to extend the waiting period to receive even greater rewards down the road. Mischel documented his findings and left it alone for the next decade or so.

He got back in touch with his subjects when the kids had grown up, either graduating high school or in their first years of college. Mischel noticed certain patterns emerging. The kids who had delayed gratification uniformly had higher SAT scores and were attending better colleges. The kids who began playing with their treats immediately ended up having lower SAT scores on average and even reported less satisfaction with the state of their lives.

Now, despite the lack of universality in the experiment, psychologists agree that delayed gratification is a significant indicator of future success. You can understand this intuitively. For example, let's say you walk past a store that displays a great pair of shoes. If you're tight on cash, do you still buy the shoes, or do you decide to create a plan to buy them in the future? Most people do neither. They remind themselves of the money they lack and beat themselves up for not fulfilling their potential, and do nothing to erase the gap in their lives. They're not to blame for this. After all, no one has shown them that it is possible to tap into that immense dormant potential.

I want to tell you that you can achieve everything you desire. All you need to learn is the correct process, and it's not as complicated as you might make it out to be. Decide which direction you want to go, and start moving that way while remaining present. That's all it boils down to. However, the ego and our environment complicate matters and can lead us astray. This is where a crucial innate quality of yours comes to the rescue.

Grit

What is grit? Well, not the stuff you put on your driveway to melt snow! I'm talking about the innate emotional quality we all possess. You might not think of yourself as tough or resilient because you haven't been put in a position where it's necessary. But, to achieve your goals, you'll need to use all the grit that you can summon up.

Think about this for a moment: If someone asks you to

complete a challenging task, do you respond with: "I'll do my best" or "I'll do it"? If, like me, you have often responded with the first option, your intentions are good - but your self-image might be lacking. You want to deliver the work on time, but you're hedging your bets before you even begin. By promising to give it your "best," you're telling yourself and the other person that if you can't deliver, it isn't your fault. After all, you gave it your best.

This is definitely a way of playing it safe. However, if you use this often, you're never legitimately challenging yourself. Not only that, but using "maybe" or "I'll try" creates this convenience by which you make yourself unaccountable for your mistakes and failures. It keeps you in a place of comfort and stability; yet, it lies embedded in complacency and stagnancy.

So, what does giving your "best" mean to you? If you were on the other side of the question, asking someone to complete a task for you, wouldn't you expect them to deliver their best just by default? So why even mention that you'll give it your "best"? The fact is that grit is one of the most significant indicators of success in life. Angela Duckworth, a psychologist from the University of Pennsylvania and an expert on the value of grit, considers it the easiest way to determine the degree of success someone will achieve in life.

Our social and education systems usually prioritize IQ in students, which is another way of saying that what we're born with determines what we will be capable of achieving. You've already learned why this is highly debatable. Research into the growth mindset has repeatedly proven that our success in life is directly proportional to the amount of work we're willing to put in.

It appears that Professor Duckworth's research revealed similar results. She has studied individuals from all walks of life, students to working professionals, and found that the degree of grit they possessed was a great indicator of their likelihood of success.

The good news is that grit is a skill that can be learned. If you're sitting there thinking about all of your mishaps and failed ventures, don't worry! We can turn it around; you just haven't learned the right information yet.

Being gritty begins with understanding that the knowledge of grit by itself helps you become grittier. As a first step, you can bring more awareness to your actions and remind yourself to stick to your tasks for more extended periods of time, whether through success or adversity. This means teaching your brain to seek out solutions and to persevere. Next, when you're ready, set up situations where you can achieve small wins.

By all means, don't look at your biggest goals and try to solve all your issues at once.

Instead, break it down into small parts, as little as possible. This way, you'll be able to achieve wins and build momentum. The positivity generated from this will fuel you even more and help you get gritty during challenging situations. Often, what we need most are positive feedback and a little encouragement. This is why it's vital for you to set up your tasks in such a way that you need to stretch yourself just past your comfort zone to complete them.

Our minds love being comfortable, and you'll be tempted to rest on your laurels. Instead, seek to expand your comfort zone and start trying to dip your toes into the unknown. Allow yourself to try new and different things! Allow yourself to experience new things, to learn from your mistakes, and to grow mentally stronger. Human beings are happiest in pursuing goals, so build on your small wins and keep pushing yourself further and higher!

Next, being gritty will require you to use your willpower, which is a very overlooked personality trait.

Using Your Will

Talk of will, and most people think of the struggle. That isn't wrong, but there are some subtleties you should recognize. Your will is a muscle just like those on your body. It gets stronger with constant use, but it also becomes weak or damaged with overuse or on tasks it's not strong enough to handle. Imagine going to the gym on your first day and lifting the heaviest weight you can find. You'll likely injure yourself and will never want to go back since the experience will have been entirely negative.

Similarly, many people rush into this process and do too much too soon. They want to get there as quickly as possible since they cannot delay gratification. At some point, their intuition and body tell them they're going too fast. Instead of listening to themselves, they use their willpower to ignore these calls thinking it's weakness speaking. As a result, they suffer from burnout.

Not only are they exhausted from doing too much, but they're also exhausted from exercising their will against themselves. It's no wonder that so many get exhausted and don't have any energy left to carry out the tasks that are relevant to their goals. So what should you be doing instead?

For starters, you need to use your will to help you combat any external difficulties that arise in your journey towards your higher self. You should never deploy your will against your intention or your inner voice. At first, it'll be hard to tell voices apart. However, make a judgment as best as you can and look at the feedback you receive. As I explained earlier, if you feel even more tired or exhausted, you're probably going against your intuition. If you feel energized, you've made the right decision to stop working for now and relax.

Since willpower is like a muscle, it's best used in short bursts. You want it to help you make that final leap that will ensure you complete your task, as opposed to helping you complete the entire task from the first step. If you're feeling a ton of resistance towards completing a task, you need to ask yourself whether your intuition is trying to tell you something or whether your ego is intervening. Taking baby steps towards achieving your objective is a good way to move forward, in sync with feedback.

Preparing ahead of time and prioritizing your tasks will help you mentally prepare for what's to come. This way, you won't have to depend on your willpower to get you through. Use techniques such as visualization and positive affirmations to prepare your mind ahead of time, and you'll find that you'll be able to call upon your willpower to overcome those final hurdles that are troublesome.

Listening to Yourself

Many philosophers and spiritual teachers have said that the easiest way to live life is to listen to yourself. This is what allows you to flow along the path of least resistance. What is the path of least resistance, and how do you step onto it? Let's begin by trying to define what the path is. The path of least resistance is one where everything simply flows for you. It doesn't mean you won't face obstacles, but you'll manage to make progress no matter how high the odds are stacked against you.

The most crucial aspect of the path of least resistance is the feeling it produces in you. Despite working hard or working long hours, you won't feel as if you're "hard at work." It merely becomes an extension of your existence. Do you ever feel you're "hard at breathing?" Hopefully not! Your brain automatically focuses on the tasks in front of it, and time seems to fly. In the long run, the path of least resistance will lead you right to your higher self.

If you're worried about the gap between your current and your highest potential self, chances are that you're not following the path of least resistance. Our minds are well attuned with who we truly are and what satisfies us. Anytime you begin to diverge away from that ideal, it lets you know. This manifests as insurmountable resistance or as a feeling of stress and unhappiness. Have you ever tried working at a task where your brain simply refused to focus? Amongst other factors, that's one way to know you've strayed away from your path of least resistance.

Everyone is unique, and therefore, everyone's path of least resistance is different. However, most of us have in common that we move more effortlessly forward when we take small steps towards our goals. Being on the path doesn't mean you won't have to worry about stress or negative emotions. That's not what this is about. Negative emotions play an essential role in our lives. They are important reminders of what we should be doing and where we should be heading – as per our own higher self. Think of it as you driving along a smooth road. If you begin to drift off and divert your trajectory, the path turns bumpy and uncomfortable, signaling you to get back on track. That's what negative emotions do. They're just as much a part of you and as important as positive emotions are.

Learning to Listen to Yourself

It sounds easy to say that you should listen to yourself,

but it is a tricky behavior to put first or make your default plan of action - especially with so many external influences! As children, we had no problems listening to our inner voice, and this is because we didn't know different. We simply went with the flow, believed in the things done for us by grown-ups, and adapted to our environment. As we grew up, we began buying into ideas and beliefs that weren't true to who we are, simply because it looks good or might seem better than what we have now. Staying true to yourself can become a constant uphill battle, full of second-guessing and doubt, not unlike climbing a steep mountain alone without a harness.

Learning how to listen to yourself is a matter of repetition and observing feedback. For example, at the gym, you would surely pay attention to the feedback your body is giving you. For mental wellbeing, feedback comes in the form of emotions and thoughts. As you begin to listen, your mind will recognize this and lead you to begin making choices that are more in line with who you are.

This is when you can begin to truly explore further and decipher your purpose[1]. What were your hopes and dreams when you were five, ten, or fifteen years old? Your ideals back then might not seem practical today, but examining the essence behind your wants at a time of innocence, openness, and opportunity could lead to something untapped within you. What was it that appealed to you most about your dream job at the time? For example, if you wanted to be a sailor, was it being in the open water that attracted you, or the idea of exploration? As our minds aren't fully molded by societal expectations at that age, there's not much of a filter to dictate who we are and how we behave.

As adults, our conscious minds are always present to assess ideas on our behavior, attach filters, and provide judgment. Don't take this as your conscious mind working against you. It's simply doing what you've been unconsciously teaching it. Rewire the right habits, or in this case, the ones in accordance with who you really are, and you'll find it making the world a better place for you. As you move closer towards your higher self, you'll find the gap between your potential and your current situation disappearing.

Often, we create gaps in our lives because we aim for the goals of others. For example, you might want to make large sums of money because that's what you see people doing on social media, or that's what pop culture says you need to be happy. These goals can be obtained physically, but spiritually, you'll never erase the gap. The gap exists because you've moved away from whom you're supposed to be and onto someone else's agenda.

Everyone has a talent that they're uniquely great at. What is yours? You might be tempted to say nothing, and that's OK! If it's been a while since you listened to yourself, then "nothing" is the most natural answer you will have. Take some time to think about what you enjoy doing or what most people around you come to you for. Dive deeper into those activities and get to the essence of them. That's what you truly enjoy about them.

Any activity can be molded to fit what you want to do. For example, if you're a natural explorer, you might love to travel and live an independent life away from the norm. This doesn't mean you have to work as a tour guide or a flight attendant. Those are just two options you have when it comes to careers in that field. You could also design websites or become a writer, help businesses with their social media campaigns, or run an online store. There are no limits.

As I said before, your starting point is fixed, but your end doesn't have to be. You can go in any direction your heart leads you. Your path of least resistance lies ready and waiting for you, and you'll now see that one of the easiest ways to get onto this path is to tap into a state of flow.

The Flow State

THERE'S a precise definition of what this state is, but flow is better experienced than explained. Mihalyi Cziksentmihlayi, the leading expert on the concept of flow, defines it as a level of existence where your actions play out naturally, directly from your subconscious mind, and nothing else seems to matter except the task in front of you. The experience is so enjoyable that people will continue, even if it comes at a high cost.

For example, a painter who doesn't think about what they're putting on a canvas or a musician who is entranced in feeling the music he's playing. These people aren't thinking consciously about what fits and what doesn't. They're simply listening to what's coming from within them, and they're creating from that spark.

You don't have to be a musician or an artist to achieve this state. Getting into a flow state can occur naturally, but it is also a matter of practice. For example, if you love cooking, you can practice being present and focus on the food you're making. You shut away the rest of the world and dive into the experience. If you love journaling, put pen to paper and let the words flow out with no regard to literary conventions. It doesn't matter whether you're typing, drawing, surfing, or crocheting; allow your mind to take over, and let yourself be submerged in the present moment and experience.

If you have a specific skill you're already good at, turn off all distractions and immerse yourself in the task. To achieve a flow state, it's imperative for you to remain calm and avoid sources of stress or expectation. These are impediments to the path of least resistance. The great thing about the flow state is that you won't need to use your will to remain on the path. You'll want to keep working as much as possible because it'll be as natural to you as breathing.

At some point, you might become fatigued, but it won't present itself as feeling tired. Instead, you'll be happy at what you've created and will rest peacefully. When I use the words creation or created, I'm not talking about typical creative projects such as music, art, words, or photography. All of us are creators. We design our lives for ourselves. If you work in HR for a big company, you're still a creator. Your work is your creation. Take pride and recognize it as a form of manifesting who you truly are. Perhaps your motivation comes from outside this zone. You could be driven by a desire to help other people or assist in processes that most people find tiresome. You could also be using the money you earn from your HR job to fuel more worthy passions. You don't need to write everything off in your life if you want to rise towards your best self. It's not about having a clean slate, but you do get the opportunity to choose the direction of your life path every single day. Everything is present for a reason. Recognize it and work in a state of peace and flow to move effortlessly towards where you're supposed to be.

Responsibility

You are a creator and have the power to design your own life. This power shouldn't be underestimated. Every single one of your thoughts has the ability to manifest into an event in your life. The positivity or negativity present in your life really is entirely up to you. As was once said, "With great power comes great responsibility."

So, what kind of life have you been creating? You might not be completely satisfied with the results you see in it, but this doesn't mean everything is wrong! Getting in touch with your power as a creator requires you to assume the responsibility of one. If you have a pet, you'll automatically adopt the responsibility of feeding the animal and making sure it's healthy. You'll make sure it gets adequate exercise and that it is well-rested and content. Yet, when it comes to assuming responsibility for our own lives, we rush to offload the burden onto someone or something else.

How often have you wished for something so much, only to see it go to someone else or pass you by? Such situations are tough to deal with, but they do happen. Most of us will shrug our shoulders on the surface, but deep inside, we start forming thoughts on how the world is unfair, or thinking that we're unlucky, and so on.

At times, luck and timing might play a role in our success, but it isn't something you can control. There's no point in trying to create narratives around it. Your focus must rest entirely on what you can control and take full responsibility for it. In this way, your results will be a natural consequence of your actions. This goes back to adopting a growth mindset. Remember that this strategy focuses primarily on the process rather than on the results.

Take responsibility for each and every step of the process

that you can control. This means you need to prepare, prioritize, focus, and execute each step to the best of your abilities. Seek feedback and incorporate it into your next task. This is how growth happens. Shit does happen: deal with it and move on. If you want to harness the power of creating your life as you desire, you'll have to accept the responsibility that comes with it. Accepting and acknowledging your mistakes is just as important as celebrating successes. You're more than capable of being accountable to yourself.

Expectation and Hope

Is adopting a growth mindset and taking control of your own life the ultimate solution? Well, probably not. A lot more comes into play. However, it is an enormous step in the right direction. Will you still meet with disappointment? I could say yes, or I could say no because ultimately, the way you choose to perceive a challenge is entirely your doing. Both of us could be faced with the same hurdle, yet it is our attitude that will determine if and how we overcome this obstacle.

There is no mechanism in this world that can give you every single thing you want, every single time. As we explored in the introduction, such an existence would be quite dull and stagnant indeed. So, if negative results will still occur, what is the difference between the state of accepting responsibility and rejecting it? As I've said, it comes down to how you view your results. Many people consume self-help material and begin expecting a quick fix. They visualize their future lives and "expect" it to manifest as quickly as possible.

Expectations can be very harmful as they unwittingly move you right back into the fixed mindset. They tend to lead us to evaluate our life based on the results we obtain in it and not by the amount of work or by the efficiency of our processes. Expecting specific outcomes in your life also assumes that you can somehow control your luck or that you can influence the will of others around you. This is impossible. If you expect the sun to rise from the west tomorrow, I can assure you that you'll be disappointed!

Here's an example. Let's say you help someone in need by giving them some money. This is a very generous act that can make a difference in someone's day or even life. You just never know. But if you do this with the *expectation* of them returning the favor at some point down the road, you're setting yourself up for potential disappointment. Who knows whether they'll be able to return your money to you? There's a chance you will never see this person again. You don't know whether they'll ever be able to return the favor, and you shouldn't expect them to.

Would you be able to adopt an emotional position that removes the need for results to go exactly your way? Doing this will allow you to keep an open mind and perhaps view possibilities that you had not fathomed previously. It communicates to your self-image that you're someone who will be fine no matter what your results look like. This is an extremely confident gesture that your mind will remember. It might be challenging at first, but with repetition and enforcing the right visualization, your schemas will begin to change. That's when the magic starts happening.

Hope can be a beautiful emotion to cultivate because no matter how bad your situation is or how down and out you might feel, there's always a chance that things will get better. If you help someone out who's in need, hope that they return the favor but avoid needing it from them. This way, you're setting yourself up to win no matter what. There's no question of disappointment in this picture. If they help you out, you benefit. If they don't, you're fine anyway. How can you possibly lose?

Hoping for positive results is also communicating responsibility to your subconscious. It's letting it know that you're the one in control, not luck or some external circumstances. Once you've executed your task, let go and allow the universe to take control. By communicating hope, you're telling your mind that you've done your best and are at peace with whatever happens.

Accountability is a key aspect of positive self-growth. It means you take full responsibility for your choices and realize that you have the power to change your life. No one can take that away from you, no matter how hard they try or how much they upset you.

Being accountable to yourself means being honest with what really motivates you and brings you closer to your higher self. It means monitoring your thoughts and behaviors for instances where you're being unkind to yourself – without giving yourself a free pass out of laziness!

Eliminating ***Negative Self-Talk***

I don't know about you, but I have to admit I've struggled for a long time with that noisy voice in my head. The endless stream of thoughts that flows day in and day out has accompanied me through many sleepless nights. From an early age, this chatter instilled self-doubt within me and created most of my limiting beliefs.

This voice can easily lead us astray from the present and even distort reality. It has the potential to destroy our career, our health, and our relationships. The endless narration of our existence can feel like such a burden sometimes! However, the voice you hear is not actually you. Before you panic, let me reassure you that you're not hallucinating either. This voice is part of you, but it is not your true self. Your true self is within, quiet, listening. Can you sit still and silent and observe this voice in your head that is not you?

This will take time and practice, but as you work towards finding that state of detachment from your thoughts, you will notice that you are slowly reconnecting with and settling into your authentic self. In doing this, you'll be able to witness how most of what you think is a reflection of many things, few of which are an unbiased version of reality. The truth is, we are absolute masters at lying to ourselves and creating stories around what we experience. As soon as you fully comprehend this notion, you'll experience a unique sense of freedom. We are often held captive by negative-self talk and limiting beliefs. By quieting all this unnecessary noise, you will gain clarity on what is what. Believe me; this is an absolute game changer! You will probably still hear that voice, but you'll feel empowered to dismiss what is not beneficial to your wellbeing, as well as allow yourself to dim it at any given time.

To eliminate negative self-talk, you will first need to notice what you - or rather that voice - is saying. Listen and observe, as if you were listening to a friend recount their day. Can you take note of the dialogue you are creating? No one else can hear it. This is a product of your perceptions and yours only.

Now that you understand that you create your thoughts, can you attempt to remove yourself emotionally? Can you create a space of non-judgment, openness, and acceptance? What is it saying right now? Just listen, and let it go.

Pay attention to the language you're using. Most of us exaggerate the negative and minimize the positive. For example, we're *happy* and *depressed*. We're *pleased* and *outraged*. Turning this into *overjoyed* and *sad* or *over the moon* and *disappointed* is just a matter of using different words. Your subconscious mind monitors the words and language you use.

There are a few common obstacles that we face in eliminating limiting thoughts. To begin healing and modifying embedded patterns, you can practice awareness throughout your day and monitor yourself for the different types of negative self-talk. Here's a list of habits that generate negative self-talk:

1. Mind reading - This pattern is when you assume you know what someone else is thinking and project negativity onto the situation. For example, "I know he's disappointed with me because he behaved/looked" a certain way.
2. Overgeneralization - We tend to forget that the majority of our lives are full of unknowns. If something negative happens right now, we tell ourselves that it'll continue to happen forever.
3. Exaggeration - In this pattern, we exaggerate our own flaws and minimize the ones of those around us, to our detriment. We tell ourselves this is how we are and that we'll never change, thus combining this pattern with the previous one.
4. Minimization - While we exaggerate our negatives, we tend to minimize our positive qualities. Naturally, this leads to a lopsided view of the situation and harms our self-confidence.
5. All or nothing - This pattern occurs when we chase our goals. We tell ourselves that we have to achieve the goal or else we're worth nothing. The

smallest flaws and mistakes are therefore exaggerated beyond belief and paint an unrealistic picture of our situation.

6. Assuming responsibility - This may sound like a good thing, but in the context of negative self-talk, it involves blaming ourselves for someone else's failure or outcomes that were beyond our control.
7. Labeling - Negative thoughts that come from the ego are filled with identity-driven goals. Labeling is when we seek to assign a description to every experience. More often than not, we assign negative labels to everything. For example, you don't get a promotion and think, "I'm unworthy/stupid/undeserving."

MAKE sure to watch the words you choose to describe events and feelings. Learn to monitor your thought patterns by refusing to engage emotionally. These are solid first steps in reducing the impact of negative self-talk on your psyche. You'll soon find your brain taking up the message and automatically filtering out what doesn't serve you.

14

BREAKING DOWN WALLS AND CHOOSING YOUR TRAJECTORY

> *"A bird sitting on a tree is never afraid of the branch breaking because its trust is not on the branch, but on its own wings."*
>
> — CHARLIE WARDLE

AT THIS POINT, you might feel ready to take on life head-first, acknowledging the extent of your responsibility in the outcome of your existence. But what if your mind simply refuses to allow you to do so? What if it keeps throwing challenges your way by pushing in negative thoughts? There might come a point when one might feel like there is no way up – or out. Depression and anxiety have reached epidemic levels in the world. They happen to be the most common form of mental illness in the United States, with 18% of the population suffering from this (*Facts & Statistics,* 2020).

What's more, women are twice as likely to be affected as men by an anxiety disorder.

There's still a lot of stigma surrounding seeking treatment for these conditions, which is unfortunate for those afraid of judgment, who are already in a vulnerable position. This is evident by the fact that only 30-40% of people suffering from these conditions will seek professional help. Societal narratives abound with regards to visiting a psychologist. This is especially the case for men, who are told since childhood that they need to be "tough" and to show no weakness for fear of compromising their masculinity. As for women, they are expected to be strong and take on much, much more than they should.

If left untreated, anxiety morphs into depression, which can have severe consequences. Most of us simply don't have any education with regards to dealing with these mental conditions. We turn to different sources of comfort, and many turn to alcohol and hard drugs to escape the pain. This is a quick fix, a temporary band-aid, but there is no doubt that it ultimately leads to a downwards spiral.

Stress is the place from which all forms of anxiety begins. A multitude of triggers can cause stress. For example, you might be working yourself too hard, or you might be chasing your goals a little too much without taking the time to rest and recuperate. Like many women around me, you might be struggling with a mental overload: full-time jobs, caring for children, household duties, family obligations…the list goes on.

If this sounds like you, can you still recall a time when you didn't feel so constantly overwhelmed? What were the things you enjoyed doing most? What do you enjoy doing, just for yourself? You must remember at all times that life works best when you're in a state of balance. You can only offer the best of yourself to others when your own cup is full!

Our bodies react to stress just as much as our minds do. In fact, stress begins in our mind and manifests in the body. When your brain perceives a threat, real or imagined, it immediately triggers a stress response. This is when your body prioritizes blood flow to your limbs, allows you to inhale more air (which is why you begin breathing faster), and de-prioritizes other functions such as digestion.

When your nervous system is finely tuned to react to any possible threat, you are ready to respond to the smallest noise or hint of movement in your environment. This state of being is beneficial when you're facing a physical threat. However, when the threat is a product of your thoughts (e.g., work deadlines, appointments to remember, etc.), your stress-response still occurs, but to no avail, except to hinder your psychological and physiological wellbeing. This means that your body is operating at the edge of its capacity, in fear of being harmed, for an extended period. As a result, it burns itself out, and inflammation sets in.

Remaining in this state can be extremely detrimental to your wellbeing. However, there are some ways to switch off this stress mode and trigger a relaxation response. Exercise is my number one personal go-to – an excellent outlet to burn off steam and healthily dispose of that excess energy. It allows you to focus squarely on what's in front of you instead of some imagined monster. Continuously overthinking? Run, pedal, swim faster! Moderating your breath is an excellent way of deactivating the stress response. The benefits of exercise on your mental health are too great to be ignored!

We often burn ourselves out in the name of being "motivated" or "passionate" and forget to treat ourselves kindly. We all have our limits, and these differ within every individual. Please remember to treat yourself with the same care you would a loved one. Don't be afraid to seek outside support and professional help. Most of us have access to a wide range of specialists who want nothing more than to help us reach our wellness destination.

Another noteworthy remark: it is nearly impossible to feel stressed when our breath is deep and relaxed. This is why taking a few deep breaths when in a stressful situation calms us down and allows us to focus on the task at hand. Thinking clearly and efficiently in a state of chronic stress is like swimming through mud - I wouldn't recommend it. Using all the tools we've already discussed, we must move towards a place of awareness. Noticing our mental state and moving towards a healthy and balanced one is crucial to our wellbeing.

So, what kind of a mental state should you seek to cultivate, and will you tell once you've reached it? To answer this question, we once again turn to ancient Eastern spirituality.

Three States of Mind

The ancient medicinal philosophy of Ayurveda contains many helpful tips for preventing disease and helping you live a fulfilling life. As an ancient philosophy, Ayurveda is primarily concerned with prevention rather than cure. One of its foundational principles deals with the three states of mind in which we regularly find ourselves.

The first and lowest state of mind is called "Tamas." If you were to personify this, it would be a person who doesn't exercise or even stir out of their couch as they watch TV all day.

The second state of mind is referred to as "Rajas." Here, a person is motivated to take action towards their goals and dreams, but they're doing so with anger, frustration, or fear. The best personification of this state of mind is a person who wakes up extremely early despite not having slept enough, goes hard at everything they do, and pushes through their work at any cost.

The third and highest state of being is called "Sattva." This word roughly translates to "wisdom." In this state, a person is at peace and is simply flowing. They understand how they need to work to achieve their goals and are keenly aware of their boundaries. They don't push themselves beyond their limits, and to an outside observer, it might not seem as if they're even working.

So, what do these three states of mind have to do with stress and anxiety? For starters, we usually experience all three states of mind as we go about our day. As defined by ancient spirituality, an enlightened person will remain in the highest state at all times. However, most people fluctuate between the three states mentioned above, depending on the stories they tell themselves and how they view the world around them.

What differentiates one person from another is the amount of time they spend in each state. A person who is unmotivated and lazy will spend most of their time in the first. Eventually, this person might watch a standard motivational video and move into the second state. This is when they tell themselves that they're being lazy and need to start working.

At first, working from the second state of mind is an excellent decision because your body and subconscious mind have become so conditioned to doing nothing that you need a shock to get moving. However, spending too much time in this state can lead to burnout and extreme stress.

You'll hear of entrepreneurs who claim to work 120

hours a week and state that working this hard allowed them to skip college or formal certification because of this. Whatever the degree of truth is here, don't allow extreme discourses to sweep you away from you. Some people are better suited to working long hours into the night while some work better in short bursts. Some of us are morning people, while others are the walking dead at six in the morning. Simply put, different people have different needs. You owe it to yourself to choose a lifestyle that works for you.

Now, here's how the third state comes into play. This state, characterized by wisdom, is searching to understand yourself better and figure out what suits you. Perhaps one hour's worth of focused work can be much more valuable than five hours of unfocused work that wasn't self-driven. What circumstances promote your best outcomes?

Pushing too much, too far, too soon might not be the best road for you. Can you create a balanced work-life routine for yourself? A lack of results combined with increased pressure promotes stress and constantly reminds us of the gaps in our lives. If you don't take steps to remedy these feelings, you will fall into a state of anxiety that will reinforce itself in your subconscious. Apply awareness to your thoughts as much as possible. Always monitor what you're feeling and break unhelpful patterns by questioning whether you're being kind to yourself.

When you're worried about the lack of results or the mountain of work you have left to complete, ask yourself whether you're treating yourself well. If you've been slacking off from work and ignoring your mountain of tasks, your inner voice will tell you to get back to work. If you've been spending too much time in the second state of mind, your inner voice will tell you to rest and come back later.

. . .

Dealing with Challenges

Listening to your inner voice when trying to achieve your goals isn't an easy task if you've never done it before. Your anxiety will kick in and try to get you to continue doing the same thing. This anxiety is once again the ego trying to frame an identity for itself. By identifying as a hard-working person who never sees results, whom the world is unkind to, you create an identity that it can revel in. Unfortunately, this does nothing good for you. Playing the victim is easy, but it does not bring you closer to your higher self.

This is because your higher self is a grounded state of your being. It is empowered and is the furthest thing from a victim. It understands that you're a creator. A creator who can choose their reality. How can such an entity ever be a victim? Anxiety and worry about the future are hallmarks of the ego trying to maintain its grip over you.

Make it a point to be kind to yourself whenever you feel anxiety kicking in. Instead of indulging your negative behaviors, ask yourself how you can show compassion, understanding, and empathy to yourself at that moment. It could be as simple as listening to music you enjoy, reminding yourself that everything will be alright as you remember that all comes to pass, or taking a walk in the sunshine. Whatever soothes you, make sure you indulge in it. This will help break part of the ego's hold over you.

Over time, as you keep repeating these positive behaviors, your subconscious mind will learn to listen to you and not your ego. You'll become accustomed to treating yourself well and will automatically spend more time in the highest state of mind. The more time you spend here, the better you'll understand yourself, which will only lead to more positive results.

. . .

Social Anxiety *and Self-Assurance*

Social anxiety is a growing disorder in the United States. According to research statistics compiled by the government, an estimated 7.1% of adults suffer from this condition (*Social Anxiety Disorder*, 2017). This number only accounts for those with severe cases of social anxiety and doesn't include people who neglect to report their condition. Unfortunately, many people explain social anxiety away as shyness or being socially awkward.

Dealing with social anxiety is tough because we're hardwired as social beings. Without personal connections, our mental states rapidly fall into the lowest (Tamas) state, and we can find ourselves settling into a routine with very little to no social input. The best way to deal with social anxiety is to develop confidence.

However, this is easier said than done. What is confidence, anyway? Some people say it's all about being comfortable with yourself and in your own skin. However, this isn't of much use when you don't know who you are and have repeatedly faced rejection for being yourself. Being 100% authentic in a world of judgment and strict social policies can be quite daunting.

People suffer from social anxiety for a wide variety of reasons. No matter your story, here's how you can deal with it efficiently.

Owning *Your Story*

When you think back on your life path this far, what particular thoughts come to mind? Which emotions resurface through evoking various memories?

As you very well know, life is filled with ups and downs. However, we often adopt a helpless attitude when life hits us with the unexpected. We conveniently fall back into playing the victim and ignore our choices in any given situation. It's easy to feel sorry for yourself and hope that someone will rescue you or even build a wall of protection to keep others away. But the world needs more people living according to their highest and truest self, and playing the victim has no place in that!

When you get down to it and observe, you'll find that confidence is deeply rooted in our willingness to be vulnerable. Can you own up to the fact that something is bothering you, yet refuse to let it define you? At one point or another, all of us face large issues in our lives. You might fall into the trap of allowing some of these issues to define who you are instead of seeing them as occurrences that happen to be taking place, momentarily, in your life.

Vulnerability might not strike you at first as being a source of strength. Indeed, we mostly think of "protect" when we hear the word vulnerable. However, a person who has owned up to their vulnerabilities and fully accepts them is the strongest person in the room. It's impossible to hurt such a person or embarrass them. After all, how can you negatively affect someone who openly admits to their flaws?

A lot of social anxiety is rooted in our desire to appear perfect, as being someone who has everything figured out. Currently, this is often reflected by impossibly attractive and (to all appearances) successful people on social media. Do you marvel at the hundreds or thousands of likes and the validating comments they receive on their posts, and the gorgeous places they always get to travel to at seemingly no expense? Perhaps. These things play tricks on your mind. I'm sure you know, deep down, that what you see is staged. Take a deep breath and remember: none of this is real!

A "perfect" person living a "perfect" existence would be

the worst possible thing you could witness, and it's also completely unrealistic. Much like living a life without challenges, there's no way such a person could ever attain their higher state of being and reach fulfillment in life this way. A person without vulnerabilities or flaws isn't a human being. They're a caricature. It's our flaws that make us unique. If the leaning tower of Pisa stood straight, it would be just another nondescript building blending into the busy city. If the Sphinx's nose weren't broken, it would be just another installation discarded by a lost civilization.

Perfection is unattainable in our lives, as you already know. When you're in a social situation, let go of the need to be perfect and just do your best. Maybe you'll come to realize that this is also what everyone else is trying to do. Be kind to yourself and remain loyal to who you are. If you have an opinion that offers support and positivity, share it. We live in an abundant world, and one thing we will never have too much of us kindness. Despite there being some less favorable situations, there are far more positive things about your existence.

Would you walk into a picturesque valley and complain that the rainbow isn't colorful enough? Stop indulging in negativity and recognize the truth of your existence. Your flaws are what make you perfect. Accept how you feel, be kind to yourself, and express yourself authentically. It takes practice to behave this way – keep trying. Like everything else, you need to repeat your new behaviors until they install themselves deep into your subconscious.

Impostor Syndrome

Our minds are curious things. We can have the ability, the experience, and even the competence to carry out a particular task, but our mind likes to say, "you're not good enough." In personal relationships, it might echo that your partner deserves better than you and that he or she is way out of your league. At work, it'll tell you that you're under-qualified for a job you've earned. If you work for yourself, you'll feel like a fraud when you try to convince prospective clients that you're perfect for the job.

Impostor syndrome is a well-known psychological phenomenon that researchers don't yet fully understand. Then again, there's a lot about our minds that we cannot comprehend. It seems to strike people who are highly intelligent and tend to be analytical. These people spend a lot of time dissecting problems and developing creative solutions, but ironically, this ability turns against them when they evaluate themselves.

The reason is that an analytical mind is geared towards identifying flaws in a problem. Think of an engineer who is designing a bridge. Every step of the way, he needs to figure out the effects of nature and other forces that might test the bridge, just to make sure it stands tall for decades to come. Ignoring any potential flaw can result in an unstable structure that creates untold damage and risks human life. This type of thinking will be highly useful to him when he designs a bridge.

However, the same reasoning will work against him when he analyzes himself to convince his boss that he deserves a raise. He will automatically look at why he shouldn't be given a raise. Ironically, he does this in an effort to put himself in his boss' shoes. But by trying to relate to what his boss sees, he's simply reinforcing his negative qualities within his subconscious. As you can see, this is a highly imbalanced view of oneself.

The engineer will have negative qualities, but he also has

countless positive ones that make him perfect for the job. Ultimately, every time you step out into the world, people treat you as you treat yourself. This doesn't mean that you should routinely ignore the negatives and only focus on the positive. Instead, you might try to stop taking yourself so seriously. Treat life and your choices as a lighthearted game. Adopt the approach of asking yourself, "what's the harm in this?" and also, "how would I react if someone else did or said this?" By deflating the seriousness of the situation, you're slowly breaking your negative pattern.

Have you seen those movies where the protagonist doesn't care about the outcome and manages to achieve things beyond their dreams? That's not exactly what you want to shoot for, but it's close. Not caring isn't a realistic approach to adopt. Instead, remind yourself that you'll be just fine no matter what happens. Use that beautiful, overanalytical brain of yours to help yourself!

In any given situation, you can ask yourself: "What's the worst that could happen? If the other person says "no" or if you receive a negative result, is your life finished as you know it? Will this problem matter two, five, or even ten years from now? What were you worrying about at this instant, ten years ago? Is it still a problem? What were you worrying about five months ago? Five years ago? Five weeks ago? You'll notice that most of your problems were not, in fact, as important as they appeared.

Life is unpredictable and will continue to throw many things your way. We tend to focus on the bad because of our negative bias, but many good things come our way as well. Restore the balance in your mind and repeatedly strike your feelings of unworthiness with reminders of the truth of the world.

JOMO

"FOMO," or fear of missing out, is one of the most deep-seated worries we have. We look at people around us living incredible lives and partaking in things that seem amazing, and we want it for ourselves. FOMO is the negative side effect of wanting to fit in. We're social creatures because imitating the actions of those around us gives us a sense of belonging. This is why your brain pressures you to replicate the choices of those around you.

Having a fear of missing out isn't always a bad thing. For example, you could see an inspirational story of weight loss and use it as inspiration to change your habits and get healthy. However, it has adverse side effects as well. You might see all of your friends posting pictures of their families, cute kids, and big homes and think that you're less somehow because you don't have anything close to those things. It will keep you in a state of dissatisfaction, always yearning to be part of something that is happening more or less in parallel with your life. FOMO makes the perceived gap between what you have and what you want feel far wider than it actually is.

Media really does intensify our feeling of missing out, but its use to drive people's behavior isn't a new thing. Advertisers have long used FOMO to entice people to buy their products. Given that it's such a rooted evolutionary response, breaking FOMO's hold on you isn't going to be an easy task, but it's far from impossible.

One way to move away from this fear of missing out is through adopting JOMO - the joy of missing out. This is another example of how you can break the negative behavior pattern in your life, mainly through practising mindfulness and gratitude. Being alone is often equated with being lonely. However, there's a huge difference between the two states of being. If you can learn to be alone without feeling lonely, you won't feel the need for extrinsic factors to build you up or complete you. It's normal to feel lonely from time to time, especially with isolation measures now being systematically imposed on us. However, you can learn to make your time alone feel like a privileged moment, a space for you to think, be authentic, and grow.

Being alone should be, more often than not, a choice. It is empowering because you're communicating to your subconscious mind that you are enough. The amount of joy you get from a situation isn't dependent on anything or anyone other than yourself. Choosing to be alone is a powerful action because you genuinely free yourself up to experience everything the world has to offer. I'm not saying that you should embrace being alone all the time. Instead, let go of the need for you to have company every time you do something. Enjoy missing out!

If you look around, you might notice that a large number of people choose poor company and unworthy friends, just to avoid being alone. They're so uncomfortable being with themselves that they'd rather spend time with people who don't have their best interests at heart. It isn't just friends either; some people jump into romantic relationships and partnerships because of the stigma of being "single." Many people feel as if they must be in a relationship and do all the things that couples do in order to fit into what is expected. You might want to stop and think about the people you are letting into your close circle. These are the people you will turn to for help, support, and guidance. They are the ones who should accept you for who you are, no matter what. Now, does this reflect the members of your tribe?

A life well-lived is spent achieving the things that speak to you personally. It's about fulfilling the mission you have in your soul, the one that aligns with your purpose. It is what lights you up and keeps you moving forward. This is what attracts people to you. If you are attracting toxicity, you should perhaps reconsider what you are putting out there. Are you a loyal supporter of your uniqueness?

Independence is something that every human being desires, and we recognize it when we see it in someone. A truly independent person isn't someone who doesn't want people. They just don't *need* others to validate their sense of self-worth. Here's an experiment you can conduct right now. Say no to a social appointment you don't want to go to but feel like you have to show up for. Now, don't make excuses! You are fully entitled to be uninterested, tired, or even having an off day. This is a part of self-care. If your best friend told you she'd had a horrible day at work and needed some time alone, would you push her to go to a dinner party she wouldn't enjoy? I'm hoping you would choose to act in your friend's best interest, as you should do for yourself.

Think of something that you've always wanted to experience but haven't been able to. For example, have you ever wanted to travel to a particular place but haven't done so because you haven't found anyone to go with? Go ahead and book that trip. See a movie by yourself. Book a table for one at a restaurant and enjoy your meal quietly and mindfully. Do what's valuable to you and dare to do it alone. You're not missing out on anything, except getting better acquainted with your beautiful self.

Time is the only resource in our lives that we never get back. The present moment is ending, and once it passes, it's gone forever. One day you'll run out of time, as will everyone else you know. At that moment, it's unlikely you'll remember the experience you had with someone whose company you didn't enjoy. You're more likely to recollect the moments that brought you profound joy, where you stayed true to yourself and pushed your boundaries.

How many truly memorable experiences are you denying yourself because of your need to have someone tag along? How many experiences are you saying no to because you're afraid of missing out on what others are doing? Embrace the joy of missing out. Be equanimous to being left out of other people's plans and lives. You are now ready to whittle your life down to what's most important.

The people who truly respect and value you will show up and support you for those important (and less significant) moments. You're never going to miss out on anything as long as you stay true to yourself. Instead of chasing moments, think in terms of attracting them into your life. Stop chasing those popular photo locations and the ideal influencer lifestyle. Who knows if they even appeal to your higher self?

Relax into who you are right now and do the things that matter most to you. You'll naturally begin to attract what appeals to your higher self, along with people who value the same things or who complement your personality. This is how you build a life that is worth living. This is how you grow stronger.

15

EMBRACING A PATH OF RESISTANCE

> *"When the roots are deep, there is no reason to fear the wind."*
>
> — *African proverb.*

It's normal to wish for a life of ease that doesn't consist of any problems. However, you've already learned that not only is such a desire unrealistic, it's also not something to aim for. A person who doesn't face obstacles in their life will never be able to rise to their highest ability. They'll never evolve to become someone greater than who they are now.

Just as metal needs to go through fire to become stronger, you need obstacles to develop your body and mind. If you want to become fit and healthy, you'll need to test yourself with physical activity regularly. Surmounting obstacles to grow stronger is a law of nature.

Despite this universal law, it remains in our nature to wish for obstacles to magically disappear instead of seeing them for what they truly are.

Every human being has the ability to recognize the innate potential of surmounting problems. In fact, we perceive deep within us that problems are challenges. They're meant to get us figuratively walking towards higher paths. As with everything else, you have a choice when it comes to facing obstacles and resistance in your life. You can either rail against it or work with it.

Challenges

For your life to flow, you need to embrace the path of least resistance. Yet, your path of least resistance will still contain obstacles. A path with no obstacles is pure fiction. After all, have you ever noticed how seemingly chaotic nature is? One of the secrets to being happy in life, and finding your passion, is to do things that present challenges to overcome. This will undoubtedly energize you and help you grow.

WHAT KIND of challenges you ask? Well, the choice is yours, so it all depends on the type of outcomes you want. However, make sure to direct your focus on things that really matter; don't lose focus over your end game. As Tony Robbins says, "Where focus goes, energy flows." People with resources and clearly defined goals value their time. This is why they tend to have an army of support surrounding them, taking care of the tasks that drain them and don't add value to their purpose. But if you don't have considerable resources, this doesn't mean you shouldn't value your time.

The universe works on an action-reaction basis, as Sir Isaac Newton proved.

Can you begin valuing your time and prioritizing the challenges you would like to overcome? Are you able to minimize your dealings with the challenges that drain you without being of service to the attainment of your objectives? If you can eliminate them altogether, then great! If you can't, see how you can reduce your time spent on them. There is always a solution to overcome obstacles, so make sure you explore all methods of minimizing undesirable challenges. What about the desirable ones, though? What should you do with those big problems that energize you and help you grow?

Gratitude

Most of us deal with so many uninspiring tasks that we can easily forget what it's like to be genuinely energized by a challenge. As a result, we treat every challenge in the same way. If you feel like you'd rather live without any obstacles, then the odds are that you're dealing with too many uninspiring situations in your life. Try to recall the information we discussed in previous chapters regarding finding your purpose and moving towards your vision. As you begin to take action on those, you will find that the following steps will flow naturally. Remember that you will meet with hurdles as you move towards your higher self. You just want to make sure the hurdles you're facing are beneficial to your growth.

Here's a thought experiment for you to consider: What's the difference between a successful, happy person and one who views themselves as unsuccessful and unhappy? Don't answer right away; take some time to think about it. As we've previously stated, a successful person will deal with their problems with a different attitude than the latter. Success does not lie in the "what," but rather in the "how."

People value different things, and their attitude towards their problems is what defines their success. Successful people have trained their abilities over many years and have grown accustomed to overcoming challenges through positivity. This doesn't mean that their challenges will end at some point. Right until the day they pass away, challenges will remain with them, just as yours will stay with you.

I strongly encourage you to recognize the value of these challenges. The appearance of a challenge on your path could be a sign that you are ready to grow stronger and to become greater than you currently are. Much like a baby is prompted to take his first steps, you're being pushed to develop your abilities and live up to your potential.

Instead of railing against obstacles and wishing them away, learn to embrace resistance through patience and gratitude. These two elements make it possible to create absolutely anything you want. You are both the writer and the protagonist in the story of your life. The power to remain stagnant or to generate change is in your hands. Can you see that this is what the obstacles and challenges in your life do for you? They're empowering you to fend for yourself and create the life of your dreams. You don't need to depend on someone else to give you all the things you want; you can create them yourself. A challenge is what helps you build your skills to do this.

So, embrace them with gratitude and recognize the role they're playing in your life. Instead of wishing them away and wanting everything to fall into your lap automatically, recognize that you're strong, and this is why you're facing a challenge. You're not helpless, far from it. Whatever you perceive today as holding you back might be the key to unlocking your full potential. If you feel helpless, it's because you're choosing to ignore your considerable power. Don't let yourself be a victim. Choose to be a survivor and a winner.

Remind yourself of your existence's unbiased truth as you conquer your limiting beliefs and move towards your highest self. Embrace all of your challenges with the gratitude they deserve; be thankful for the opportunities they bring about. In fact, instead of wishing for better times, create them by taking on greater challenges. After all, that's how you'll grow and become unstoppable.

*How Gratitude Changes **You***

Gratitude has long been mentioned as a means of achieving greater states of happiness and satisfaction in our lives by ancient philosophy and spirituality. These days, scientific evidence backs up this notion. Research shows that people who express gratitude experience more positive emotions, are more likely to be forgiving, empathic, and are also less likely to prioritize materialistic goals (Craig, 2019).

The most potent effect of practicing gratitude is allowing you to realize that you create the world you live in. What I mean is that you'll be far more aware of the choices you make every day and their effect on your state of mind. No matter the resistance you experience or the challenges you face, adopting an attitude of gratitude helps you deal with them much more effectively. By reframing your obstacles as challenges that will help you grow, you'll be in a better state of mind to deal with them.

So how can you go about practicing and adopting gratitude? One way to do this is to maintain a gratitude journal. At the end of each day, take a few minutes to write down at least five things for which you're grateful. If you find this to be a difficult task, begin by thinking about the things that went well for you or what you feel good about, instead of trying to "qualify" something as being worthy of gratitude.

For example, you can be grateful for your health. If you're healthy, you're in a great spot to make changes in your life. Imagine being sick and how much that would debilitate you. Good health is one of the best gifts that nature can give you, so be thankful for it. You can give thanks for being alive. As long as you're breathing, you're important, and you matter in this world. You have the power to change your life, no matter how insurmountable the odds might seem.

If you have clean water and healthy food to eat, give thanks for this as well. The more you begin to notice the little things that are right in your life and how special they are, the better you'll feel. And while you're at it, it wouldn't hurt to pay yourself a compliment at the end of each day!

Many of us are quick to compliment others and admire them, but we rarely take the time to pat ourselves on the back and congratulate ourselves on a job well done. We tend to do this only when we're exhausted and want to take a break. We recognize our value when we're about to burnout. Why not be gentler and compliment yourself at the end of your day? Be thankful for how far you have come from this time last year. Recognize how good of a job you did today, with any challenges you faced.

By focusing on the positive in this way, you'll begin to change the way your brain is wired, and real changes will follow. The more positive your outlook is, the less stress you'll experience in your life, and the attendant health benefits of this are huge. Did you know that stress tends to produce a biological reaction called inflammation in our bodies?

Inflammation is a natural bodily response to threats. For example, if you cut your finger, the area on the cut will swell and turn red. The skin around the wound will become tender. You might wrap it up in a bandage and seek to avoid using that finger for the rest of the day. Your brain is engineering your bodily response to this situation because it's diverting resources towards that part of your body to heal the wound. Inflammation is what drives this kind of messaging and gets you to stay out of the body's way as it heals.

As useful a process as this sounds, too much inflammation is a bad thing (Snyder, 2015). When your body is inflamed, it's in a state of stress. However, the relationship works the other way as well. If you experience chronic stress, your brain is likely to think it's under attack and will activate an inflammatory response. This will kick your body's defenses into high gear. Except, there's no wound or disease to fight. It's all in your head.

Without anything to fight and thanks to being constantly required to protect you against an invisible threat, your body begins to turn on itself. This is what causes a group of diseases called autoimmune diseases. Of course, stress is not the only cause, but it is proven to play an important role. Arthritis, cancer, lupus, and multiple sclerosis are examples of autoimmune diseases. They have no cure yet, and all of these diseases feature the body turning its natural abilities against itself.

Your body can replicate its cells when old ones die, and this function is essential for life. However, if it goes rogue and new cells are formed without old ones dying, a tumor forms, which can be fatal to your health. Many other conditions result in cancer propagating through someone's body, but inflammation is where it all begins. Stress causes inflammation, but positivity and gratitude kill stress.

This is why gratitude has a significant impact on physical and mental wellbeing. Practicing gratitude is a skill that can be learned. Make it a point to maintain a gratitude journal and to seek the positive in yourself every day; you will soon find you've developed a new, life-changing habit.

The Problem-Solving Mindset

Because of our inbuilt negativity bias, we are inclined to focus on problems rather than solutions. This creates stress within our bodies, and it can be tough to snap out of it. It would be too tricky to attempt to rewire your brain to weigh the positive as much as the negative. This is an evolutionary bias we have, and undoing it completely might prove more harmful than useful.

Instead, it's best to work with the negativity bias to reframe the challenges you face in life. The way to do this is to adopt a problem-solving mindset. This mindset acknowledges that a problem or harmful condition exists. It then pivots your mind to focus on the solution to the problem instead of imposing a positive solution on top of it. In this way, you can regulate your emotions and push yourself to overcome your challenges.

The best way of regulating your emotions is to enforce rationality in a situation. I'm not suggesting you become a robot or an automaton. Instead, remind yourself of what is true at the present moment and act on that basis. The present moment might present a huge set of challenges, so focus on solving the problem instead of diverting your focus to the problem itself.

So how can you enforce rationality in a situation? Let's

consider an example where you find yourself having limiting thoughts about a situation. Here's a handy list of questions you can ask yourself to get your mind to think about the challenge objectively:

1. Is there substantial evidence that supports my negative thoughts?
2. Is there any evidence against them?
3. Am I interpreting the situation with all the available evidence?
4. What would a friend say about this situation and my thoughts?
5. How can I view this situation positively?
6. Will this matter in five years? Ten years?

RUNNING your thoughts through a quick checklist of questions will pull your mind out of the negative spiral, and you'll be able to regain control over them. Practice this method often enough, and your brain will begin to kick in automatically.

Rationality is cold-blooded and is squarely focused on the present moment. There's no room for time traveling or identity building, which is what the ego loves to do. By remaining focused on the present moment, you'll defuse the emotional situation and regain control of your mind. Through repetition, this will become a habit that your subconscious mind will carry out automatically.

16

EMBARKING ON YOUR JOURNEY

> *"The meaning of life is just to be alive. It is so plain and so obvious and so simple. And yet, everybody rushes around in a great panic as if it were necessary to achieve something beyond themselves."*
>
> — ALAN WILSON WATTS

NO MATTER THE trajectory you intend to give your life, we all need, at one point or another, to stop planning and contemplating and just make it happen. Expanding your knowledge is a significant first step, but it's only a small part of the process. Taking action, incorporating feedback, re-educating yourself, and moving forward with passion, grit, perseverance, and positivity will make up most of your journey.

It might be intimidating at first, but do whatever you can in the present moment. If I've learned anything by now, it's that with patience and passion, the sky is the limit. Remind yourself that good things - and great things - really do take time. Choosing to start your journey, whether now or tomorrow, is of extraordinary value – just keep showing up for yourself.

Achieving success isn't about carrying out some grand plan that you think up late at night, nor is it about coming up with something so mind-bogglingly original that no one will know what to think. Sure, innovation and creation are part of the process, but they aren't central to success, nor to your personal development. The core lies in regular action. Keep doing the little things, and make this a consistent effort. You'll get the results you seek; this is the essence of the growth mindset, after all.

When you first start, your ego will prompt you to look at all the work and hurdles ahead of you. It'll highlight the gap between your current existence and your goals. It will make you wonder how you could ever make anything considerable happen. If you aren't careful, you'll end up siding with your ego. However, if you've read up to this point, you now understand that giving up is only an idea because if you keep showing up and trying, you are telling your mind that you are winning.

Understanding the various little tricks that the ego plays is as much a part of success as taking action. Adopt the principle of doing something, however little it may seem, whenever you can. Don't worry about achieving larger goals right away. Keep taking baby steps towards your vision and move forward. Once you begin doing this, your ego will shift to how long it will take you to get to where you want to be. Before you know it, you'll look back and realize you've actually come quite a long way.

And what about those negative beliefs and hindering

thought patterns you've nurtured for so long? The ones that like to remind you that you're not doing enough and that your goals are unachievable? Well, what if someone else was telling your best friend that they're not capable of reaching their objectives? That they are too lazy or incompetent? Your reaction should be shock and outrage. You know what this "friend" is capable of when she or he sets their mind to it. You are your own best friend. Believe in yourself and be your number one supporter. That self-limiting discourse in your head is not you.

Now, you will need to learn to juggle these new habits with a healthy lifestyle to avoid burning yourself out and falling right back into old ways. Take time out of the equation by returning to the present moment. When you hear the ego begin to speak up, just return to the task at hand, and focus on completing it. Acknowledge the ego is present but pay no attention to it. Treat it as white noise and keep going back with kindness to your current task. Change the dialogue, sprinkling it with compassion and positivity. Gradually, you'll be able to tap into a state of flow and move towards your goals with seemingly less effort than before.

There are just a few more things we should discuss as you begin to move forward in your journey.

The Past and the Future

Now, for a slight twist before we conclude, let's take a look at all we've discussed so far from a somewhat different perspective.

The world of physics was in a state of major upheaval during the early 1900s. Albert Einstein provided evidence that changed the way we think of time and space. Meanwhile, Nobel Prize winner Niels Bohr also played a significant role in questioning foundational physics.

Bohr, regarded as the father of quantum physics (Aaserud, 2019), challenged the Newtonian models, which specified that the universe was fixed and that large bodies were solid. Although Newton never used these exact terms to describe his theories, it is known that this is what was implied. Bohr's work turned this model upside down.

His experiments and research focused on sub-atomic particles and their behavior under different circumstances. Bohr began his experiments assuming Newtonian laws, but he soon found himself lost in a new world that didn't behave as expected. For starters, Bohr realized that he was unable to physically observe any subatomic particles. Instead, all he saw were waves. He then realized that these waves were caused by particles that were vibrating at extremely high frequencies.

Think of it this way. Hold a rubber band between your fingers and stretch it. Now, pull the band to one side and let go as it vibrates. If you look at the rubber band at that moment, it'll seem as if it's in multiple places at once. This is because it's vibrating faster than our eyes can comprehend. It seems to move as a wave since it isn't still. Now multiply that vibration by order of a million or so to picture the behavior of subatomic particles.

What this means is that everything we see around us isn't stable but is composed of particles that are moving so fast that they appear solid to us. Perhaps you already knew that the entire universe is in constant motion. However, Bohr also found that the mere act of observing these particles changed their behavior. Interestingly, the intentions of his experiment and his assumptions always gave him the results he wanted. This was because he was affecting the behavior of these particles.

Bohr realized that when he assumed that these particles vibrated at a certain frequency, that was the frequency he would observe. If he assumed a lower value or expected something different, he would receive that exact result. This was an absolute game-changer in physics because it revealed that reality itself was apparently "untrue" or subject to the observer's intentions. So, if our perceptions can influence reality, does subjective reality even exist?

With the awareness and understanding of this concept, we can see how physics can cross over into the realm of philosophy and the Buddha's teachings about journeying within. Keeping this interconnectedness in mind, we can better observe our own vibrations and perhaps contemplate the veritable power we hold within.

CREATING ***a Future***

The renowned scientist Sir Stephen Hawking dedicated his life to developing a "Theory of Everything" but couldn't close the gap, and neither could Einstein. And then we have Bohr's work, of which the implications are massive. All distinct advancements in the field aside, theories collide where it appears that the entire universe is not fixed. Various conclusions point to the fact that we can seemingly influence our lives by setting strong intentions and living according to the principles of our ideal reality. Bohr could generate results based on his expectations, and so can you.

Now can you see how you're a creator? If you expect the worst and live your life according to the principles and beliefs of your past, you're vibrating at that frequency. If you choose to be a victim of your thoughts and circumstances, you'll generate results that validate that frequency.

But if you work to live in your ideal present, which inevitably turns into your future, you'll begin vibrating at that frequency and will create it. Time doesn't matter in the quantum realm. This is why visualization, taking action, being grateful, and setting positive intentions are so powerful. Doing them once or twice or at fixed points during the day isn't enough; they are habits that need to be continually nurtured.

To change your reality, you'll need to vibrate at your desired level at all times or as much as possible. Your ego will fight back and will drag you back into the past. Your subconscious mind, which is used to vibrating at the frequencies of the past, will agree. It is up to you to disrupt these patterns and re-educate your mind. Believe in what you want and move towards your goals. You can create your reality.

Feel free to set aside fixed times for visualization. Practice associating positive emotions to small accomplishments. You can carry your healthy mindset into everything you do! Use awareness to recognize past vibrations dragging you down, and make a conscious decision to switch back to the present.

I mentioned earlier that an attitude of gratitude is the best way of living your life. It is an easy road to contentment and long-term happiness. In one way, gratitude works because it is a show of faith in the unknown that is bringing you everything you want. In reality, you are simply revealing the abundance already present in your life. Gratitude is your pot of gold. As you slowly begin to overstep old patterns and build instinctive appreciation, you will notice more and more good things come your way. Your mind will come to detect opportunities more quickly, and your constructive growth mindset will be ready to take on all challenges on your path. Is it any surprise that you'll begin receiving the gifts of that higher self's reality in your present moment?

Trust

As you embark on this journey, many external events will force you to question whether you're doing the right thing. Your ego will undoubtedly give you a nudge when you're not vibrating at your desired frequency. Beware, this nudge will turn into a slap if you let your ego take over! It will remind you of your old ways and throw your self-limiting beliefs back in your face. If you fall for this trap, you'll begin to beat yourself up and will fall back into your negative patterns.

Instead, disrupt the ego by being kind and refusing to admonish yourself. It seems counterintuitive to do this, but it works. Rather than being disappointed that you're not feeling good emotions, remind yourself that it's okay not to feel good all the time. You are allowed to be sad, angry, and disappointed. Accept that some resistance will happen and remind yourself of the fact that you care about yourself and are moving forward no matter what. Greeting these harsher emotions is a big step towards healing and moving forward. Being kind to yourself will automatically help you process the resurfacing emotions, and you'll slowly find the resistance melting away.

The state of accepting that we don't know something is uncomfortable. How many times have you pretended to know an answer when you haven't, in an effort to avoid discomfort? Although I have a tendency to be shockingly honest (to my detriment!), this is something all of us have done at some point in our lives. How about embracing the discomfort of not knowing by putting your faith and trust in the unknown? I'm not talking about relying on some sort of spiritual hoodoo! Remember how Bohr's quantum model of physics backs up the fact that we create our reality?

Balance

Positive people maintain their outlook by following a principle of balance. Every human being needs nourishment in their professional, personal, and spiritual life. You cannot lead a happy existence without nurturing all three. A person who lives purely for their work and spirituality will feel the lack of human contact and relationships. Someone who lives solely in the spiritual and personal realm but neglects their professional life will find practical matters such as money interfering with their journey.

Balance is the key to everything. Buddha prescribed the wisdom of adopting the Middle Path as a means to living a fulfilling life. This doesn't mean living a neutral life or never believing in anything. Nihilism is far from what Buddha was talking about. Instead, it's about finding balance in everything. Be passionate about what you love whilst recognizing that alternate views exist. The existence of alternate views doesn't negate your reality, nor does it diminish your beliefs and choices.

These days, social media has removed all semblance of balance in world views. It seems as if everyone has to belong to one side or another. These sides consume information that appeals to them (once again in correlation with the confirmation bias) and refuse to engage with differing opinions or even consider the existence of other points of view. As a result, they live in self-sustaining thought bubbles. When anyone approaches with an alternative viewpoint, they react aggressively and with outrage instead of engaging with one another calmly.

Would you be able to monitor your language for the presence of extreme words? Do you refer to us versus them themes in your life? Is there balance in the information you consume and where you source this news? To move forward and grow as a person, it is essential to keep an open mind. Seek to engage with alternative perspectives as much as possible. Remind yourself that your reality is solely yours and not under the influence of someone else. Therefore, your world view isn't the only truth. Every one of us on this planet is living multiple realities that are unique to ourselves. You don't have to understand it entirely, but you do need to acknowledge it.

You might fall into the YouTube motivational speaker's trap where they'll convince you that you're lazy and need to work all the time towards your goals—if that works for someone else, then good for them. Listen to yourself and respect what your body and mind tell you. Somedays, you might be able to work 15 hours straight. On other days, finding the energy to work for even an hour might be beyond you. Allow yourself to be as you are, and experience each day with a fresh, clear view. While we work towards our goals, we all need to rest and indulge in other areas of life to maintain a holistic and balanced existence.

Positive Habits

There's a lot of material out there regarding the positive habits people follow to lead productive lives. While habit stacking might feel overwhelming at first, most habits originate and develop from a feeling of responsibility and acknowledgment that you are the ultimate creator of your reality. Once you fully accept this fact, everything else in your life will follow suit. Accept full responsibility for your results and allow everything to flow.

One common trait in positive individuals is the acceptance that many things are outside their control; in other words, resilience. For example, if you work hard at a task but don't experience the success you envisioned, let go of the need for it to work out exactly as you expected. Often, the world has a better plan for you; you just need to actively seek out that open door.

Living in hope allows you to get excited about your future and also creates some space for the universe to provide you with something better. Hope can help you recognize that everything enables you to grow, no matter how negative something might seem on the surface.

Always prioritize your happiness, and don't mistake this for being selfish. If you don't take care of yourself and ensure you're functioning at your best, you're of no use to anyone else. Many people say this but fall short in terms of practicing it in their lives. They say yes to situations that don't speak to who they are, all in the name of appearing agreeable.

Behaving this way can only build frustration and resentment, and all that negative energy will eventually spill out at inopportune moments. However, you can avoid this issue entirely by drawing firm boundaries. You can only expect the world to treat you in the same way you treat yourself. Respect your time and boundaries, and the world will do the same. Sure, it'll test you from time to time, but as long as you remain firm and establish clear expectations, you'll find that you'll attract more of what you truly deserve.

Finally, try to maintain an attitude of balance with everything you do. Recognize your deep-seated power and that you really are enough – you are all you need in life. As long as you're breathing, you have immense potential and can create any reality you believe in. Live in it and bask in the positive emotion it generates. Use your will to work towards your goals and live in your best state. Trust the unknown and recognize how you're creating a new life for yourself. Opportunities are renewed every moment of every day.

Choose Your Environment

You always have a choice to believe in your vision and your reality. You can do this no matter how supportive your environment is. While you remain your own ultimate driving force and are capable of making the right choices, it's a lot easier to make the right ones when your environment is aligned with your objectives.

There's no doubt that our environment plays a huge role in creating our beliefs from a young age. Your surrounding and circumstances have the power to mold you as an adult. When you begin to live consciously, you'll find that your environment will change in accordance with who you're becoming. You can increase the degree of alignment in your life by choosing the right environment for yourself. Ensure you are fully aware of choosing who you interact with, your living situation, the city or scene you live in, the media you consume, and how you spend your time.

Seek to interact with other driven individuals, and indulge in activities aligned with your higher self. For example, if you're someone who doesn't like staying out all night and partying in the name of a good time, don't assume you need to do this. Think of your needs and try to find activities that are more in line with who you really are. Perhaps you prefer more active, artistic, or intellectual pursuits?

Your environment will always seem to be one step behind

who you're becoming during the initial part of your journey. Don't fall into the gap here. Be thankful for the beauty in what you are trying to achieve, and resolve to remain on your path no matter how many times you are diverted. It's also important to recognize that your past and current environments played a role in pushing you towards where you are now headed. Sure, it might not have been ideal. However, in some way, it did motivate you to seek change, and you're now moving towards your greater and better things.

Everything can be helpful if you allow it to be. Even the most negative situations hold significant lessons for you and can help you grow. With an attitude of openness and a resilient spirit, you can become unstoppable.

As you begin to make changes, be prepared for your current environment to challenge you. After all, resistance is a part of change! Don't get drawn into others' negative thought patterns and limiting beliefs; they are merely a projection of their own short-comings. On the other hand, you might find other relationships flourishing and even inspire some to seek out better things for themselves. If you see people close to you aren't as understanding or supportive as you need them to be, then perhaps you should ask yourself whether you truly need these individuals in your life at all.

Remember to react with compassion and care as much as you can. It might seem impossible to behave this way when someone mocks you or diminishes your dreams and aspirations. However, they're doing this from a state of fear and ignorance. You don't need to adopt a holier than thou attitude or act as if you know more than them. Realize that they are living their own reality according to their perceptions, as you are in yours. Keep your business to yourself to protect that flame burning inside you, and keep taking actions to supports your goals.

Most importantly, what this all comes down to is striving to live in alignment with your highest self. Practice gratitude and give thanks for everything in your life. Whether you know it or not, everything has conspired to place you on your path.

17

CONCLUSION

So, how do we go about growing stronger, in all aspects of our inner space? I'm positive that by this point, you've gained a good understanding of the multiple facets that come into play, as well as what it takes and what you already possess inside of you to become the best version of yourself. Remember that reading and educating yourself is only the first step. Now, it's time for you to take action towards your goals and make a lasting change. Good things really do take time, so remember to take small steps and recognise how far you've come. Do something every day, no matter how big or small, that will eventually add up to more considerable effective change.

As I've mentioned, it is essential to reflect the feeling of reaching to your higher self as you go about your day. This doesn't mean that you must constantly focus on your end goal, but rather recognize that you are on the path towards it. You will find that returning your focus to the present and to the task in front of you will be far more manageable, and in doing this you will move quickly towards your vision. Anxiety and self-doubt will rear their heads from time to time; they are part of the game, so don't expect them to be suddenly eliminated altogether. Just remember that their volume can be turned down, and the power is yours to tune them out.

After all, you're changing your well-established behavioral patterns, and these will undoubtedly put up a fight. Your body and mind have been used to a certain way of being and will naturally react to change with alarm. Keep taking bite-sized chunks out of your goals, and over time you'll condition your subconscious mind to flow according to your new ways.

When you feel anxiety or doubt creep in, take any action forward. Make sure to keep things in motion! In doing so, you will enable space to be created, allowing opportunities to present themselves. Moreover, responding to anxiety with action trains your subconscious mind to use negative emotions as fuel. The role of negative emotions is just as essential as positive ones. Unfortunately, we often misuse negative emotions, resisting and transforming them into obstacles, thus hindering our state of mind. Break that pattern now by reminding yourself to take action, rather than allowing negativity to spiral downwards. Start today: Own up to your emotional reactions and reclaim control of your thoughts as an observer.

Now, please keep in mind that it is important to connect to your guidance from the Universe (or bigger picture, if you will) because that is a huge part of releasing resistance. When you truly understand that the world around you has your back, and you can easily find guidance in knowing that **life is happening for you, not to you**, it's so much easier to shake off the distracting cynicism. You will feel the weight drop off your shoulders. Everything that comes into your life is serving you. Maybe what you are going through right now will result in some innovative creation. Maybe your hardships will be the story you use to touch and transform other people's lives, perhaps in the same way I am sharing this with you now. It is very difficult to perceive the full extent of our potential and abilities. The least we can do is learn as much as we can, grow into our best selves, and pay it forward - share the love!

As beings made of energy we are all connected. Everything we see in others is already within us. You might not like someone in a specific moment because they are clearly putting on a facade or acting as if they are better than someone else. This acts as a trigger because that trait might be something unpleasant you recognize in yourself. So, when you find yourself in this situation, stop and ask yourself, "what is it I see in this person that is eliciting this negative response?"

This can go the other way, too. Say you really look up to a friend because they run a successful business, and they are full of love, kindness, and empathy, and you really admire their impact on your life. The only reason you can recognize those qualities in them is that they are already part of you. You can only rarely see something in another person that is not already, in some way, within yourself. Find a way to be what you wish to see in others, and to exhibit and reflect what you want out of life.

On a final note, here's a reminder: *Everything you put out comes back,* and the way you love yourself reflects the standard to which others will be held. As you align your actions and thoughts with whom you want to become, everything around you will begin to shift. It is normal to feel intimidated and look into the distance from where you are to where you want to be and wonder how you're going to make it. Again, remember to pace yourself and celebrate small wins! Look at it this way: If someone was to lay out all the food you're going to eat over the next year in front of you, would you be able to eat it all in one sitting? Sounds like fun, but I don't think so!

Instead, you'll eat it in small portions over time, just as you'll achieve your goals by moving in the right direction and holding firmly the knowledge that you can - and will – overcome any obstacle thrown your way. You can't expect yourself to do everything at once. You must take action, incorporate feedback, and take further action. So, settle in for the long haul! Resolve to act according to your most authentic self from here on out, if anything simply because *your happiness is worth it.*

I hope you're as excited for yourself as I am for you! I want to thank you for allowing me to be a part of your journey and for trusting me in seeking inspiration within the pages of this book. I hope you feel a little more empowered and inspired to achieve your highest goals, and to grow into the most authentic and beautiful version of yourself.

Leave a Review

As an independent author with a small marketing budget, reviews are my livelihood on this platform. If you enjoyed this book, I would truly appreciate it if you left your honest feedback. You can do this by clicking the link to the *Awakening to Authenticity Collection* on www.amazon.com .

Additionally, you can join our Facebook community here, or contact me directly via ydgardens@emeraldsocpublishing.com.

I love hearing from my readers and I personally read every single review.

Stay well & strong.

Kindly,

YasD.

Just for You

A Special Gift to Our Readers

Included with your purchase of this book is your free copy of *7 Secrets to Speaking your Mind and Standing your Ground*.

Follow the link below:
www.emeraldsocpublishing.com

ABOUT THE AUTHOR...

Y.D. Gardens is a teacher, writer, and author of *Growing Into You, Growing Stronger,* as well as *The Well-Being Handbook* (coming soon). Before immersing herself in the world of primary education, Y.D. Gardens enjoyed years of health and fitness coaching. She is an avid reader with a particular fondness for travelling, animals, yoga, ice hockey ... and cheesecake.

In creating The Emerald Society, she has combined her passion for creation, education, and physical and mental wellness. Originally from Québec, Canada, she now savours each day of her dream life along the Australian East Coast, teaching children and writing books.

Author photograph @madlovephotographer

To find out more, visit www.emeraldsocpublishing.com

ALSO BY Y.D. GARDENS

Growing Into You

Growing Stronger

The Well-Being Handbook (coming soon)

Visit www.emeraldsocpublishing.com

THE EMERALD
SOCIETY

REFERENCES

Aaserud, F. (2019). Niels Bohr | Biography, Education, Accomplishments, & Facts. In *Encyclopædia Britannica*. https://www.britannica.com/biography/Niels-Bohr

Bayes-Fleming, N. (2019, June 7). *How to Recognize and Overcome Trauma*. Mindful. https://www.mindful.org/how-to-recognize-and-overcome-trauma/

Cook, G. (2020, November 16). *Why We Are Wired to Connect*. Scientific American. https://www.scientificamerican.com/article/why-we-are-wired-to-connect

Craig, H. (2019, March 3). *The Research on Gratitude and Its Link with Love and Happiness*. PositivePsychology.com. https://positivepsychology.com/gratitude-research/

Drew, C. (2020, November 16). *Poststructuralism in Education | Theory & Examples (2020)*. Helpful Professor. https://helpfulprofessor.com/poststructuralism-in-education/

Dweck, C. S. (2016). *Mindset: the new psychology of success*. Ballantine Books.

Singer, M.A. (2007). *The Untethered Soul: the journey beyond yourself*. New Harbinger Publications and Noetic Books.

Facts & Statistics. (2020). Adaa.org. https://adaa.org/about-adaa/press-room/facts-statistics

Hanson, R. (2009). *Buddha's Brain: The Practical Neuroscience of Happiness, Love and Wisdom* (1st ed., Vol. 1). New Harbinger Publications. (Original work published 2009)

Ho, L. (2020, March 20). *Conscious Mind vs Subconscious Mind: How to Improve Them?* Lifehack. https://www.lifehack.org/868323/conscious-mind-vs-subconscious-mind

Maltz, M., & Kennedy, D. S. (2002). *The new psycho-cybernetics: the original science of self-improvement and success that has changed the lives of 30 million people*. Souvenir Press.

Mcleod, S. (2007, February 5). *Nature vs. Nurture in Psychology*. Simplypsychology.org; Simply Psychology. https://www.simplypsychology.org/naturevsnurture.html

Mcleod, S. (2018, June 6). *Jean Piaget's Theory of Cognitive Development*. Simplypsychology.org; Simply Psychology. https://www.simplypsychology.org/piaget.html

Mischel, W. (2014). *The marshmallow test: mastering self-control*. Little, Brown And Company.

Mueller, J. (2020, March 24). *Clear and Present Safety: The World Has Never Been Better and Why That Matters to Americans - Ethics & International Affairs*. Ethics & International Affairs. https://www.ethicsandinternationalaffairs.org/2020/clear-and-present-safety-the-world-has-never-been-better-and-why-that-matters-to-americans/

Schoen, M., & Loberg, K. (2014). *Your survival instinct is killing you: retrain your brain to conquer fear and build resilience*. Plume, Published By The Penguin Group.

Snyder, W. (2015, February 10). *The Good, The Bad and the Ugly of Inflammation*. Vanderbilt Medicine Magazine. https://www.mc.vanderbilt.edu/vanderbiltmedicine/the-good-the-bad-and-the-ugly-of-inflammation

Social Anxiety Disorder. (2017, November). Nih.Gov.

https://www.nimh.nih.gov/health/statistics/social-anxiety-disorder.shtml

The limbic system. (2019, January 24). Uq.Edu.Au. https://qbi.uq.edu.au/brain/brain-anatomy/limbic-system

Mallory, A. (2016, August 26). *Not the Mountain we Conquer, but Ourselves. New* Heights in Human Performance & Leadership. https://alanmallory.com/2016/08/not-the-mountain-we-conquer-but-ourselves/

Image References

Achieve. (2020). In *Pixabay.*

Backpacker. (2020). In *Pixabay.*

Connection. (2020). In *Pixabay.*

Dawn. (2020). In *Pixabay.*

Flow. (2020). In *Pixabay.*

Koshkina, L. (2020). Path. In *Pixabay.*

Past. (2020). In *Pixabay.*

Walls. (2020). In *Pixabay.*

Woman. (2020). In *Pixabay.*

Yoga. (2020). In *Pixabay.*

NOTES

13. Living up to Your Potential

1. The term purpose is not used here to define oneself, but rather to explore the extent of our potential in order to live a fuller and happier life.

CPSIA information can be obtained
at www.ICGtesting.com
Printed in the USA
LVHW081935060521
686674LV00002B/83

9 781922 575074